Just a Mo

Just a Mo

My Story

Laila Morse

with Rebecca Cripps

2 4 6 8 10 9 7 5 3

First published in the UK in 2013 by Virgin Books,
an imprint of Ebury Publishing

A Random House Group Company

www.randomhouse.co.uk

Addresses for companies within The Random House Group Limited
can be found at www.randomhouse.co.uk/offices.htm

The Random House Group Limited Reg. No. 954009

A CIP catalogue record for this book is available from the British Library

The Random House Group Limited supports The Forest Stewardship
Council® (FSC®), the leading international forest certification
organisation. Our books carrying the FSC label are printed on FSC®
certified paper. FSC is the only forest certification scheme endorsed by
the leading environmental organisations, including Greenpeace.
Our paper procurement policy can be found at
www.randomhouse.co.uk/environment

Typeset by E-Type

Plate section design by carrdesignstudio.com

Printed and bound by CPI Group (UK) Ltd, Croydon, CR0 4YY

ISBN: 9780753541395

To buy books by your favourite authors and register for offers, visit
www.randomhouse.co.uk

To Gary, Mum, Jackie, Tracy and Gerry

Contents

Famous, Me?

I T WAS A humid summer's evening. I was unwinding at home after a long, hot day of making deliveries in my van, when my boyfriend George turned up. The kids were at my mum's.

'Got anything planned?' George asked.

'Nothing much,' I said.

'I've got to pick up some keys from Jas in Woolwich,' he said. 'Fancy coming along?'

It wasn't much of an offer, but I'd go anywhere with George, even if it was only to his business partner's house in Woolwich and back again. I was mad about him.

Half an hour later, we arrived at Jas's house. 'My cousin's here from India,' Jas said, introducing us. 'He can tell fortunes. He reads palms.'

'Go on, then, tell my fortune!' I said, holding out my hand to him. 'Don't say a tall, dark, handsome stranger is about to come into my life, because that's already happened!' I gave George a wink.

Jas's cousin studied my palm with interest. 'Oh my God!' he said. 'You're going to become famous one day.'

'What?' I said, frowning.

He nodded vigorously. 'Yes, I can see it as plain as daylight. Everybody's going to know who you are.'

Well, you never know, I thought.

My younger brother Gary was at drama school. Perhaps,

when he graduated, he would work with a load of well-known actors. Then I might land up with one of them and marry him. I'd be famous by association, then, wouldn't I? I certainly couldn't imagine it happening any other way. I was never going to be famous in my own right.

I told a few people: 'A palm reader said I'm going to be famous one day!'

'Really?' they would say, looking at me in disbelief. 'Don't be stupid. How could *you* end up famous?'

Not one person took it seriously, not even to humour me. It wasn't even a long shot. I was a nobody and I would always be a nobody.

They're right, I thought. It's never going to happen. How could someone like me become famous?

chapter one

Little Terror

TAKING A DEEP breath, I knocked at the door of 16 Hatcham Park Road. Then I ran back outside the gate, closed it and waited.

The door of the terraced house opened. A little man appeared. He was wearing a dark suit, a black waistcoat and a false collar. A tremor of fear went through me. Peering at me through a pair of round horn-rimmed spectacles, he waited for me to speak. A lump came into my throat. All I could think of was how much he resembled the famous murderer, Dr Crippen.

'Is Primrose in, please?' I mumbled, my heart thumping.

He turned his back on me and shouted into the house, 'Primrose, you're wanted!' Then he was gone.

I stared at the ground, waiting for my heartbeat to slow. Prim appeared at the door. 'Come in!' she said, smiling her broad, open smile.

'No, your dad...' I whispered.

'Come on!' she said, turning to walk down the hall.

I stepped gingerly into the house, secretly glad that she had insisted. I preferred it when her dad wasn't there, but I still loved going to Prim's house. Although it was only three doors down from where we lived, it was like stepping into a different world.

A clock started cuckooing as I walked along the passage after Prim. Then another clock began to cuckoo, and another.

Prim's dad was always fiddling about with his collection of cuckoo clocks, which all seemed to have different chimes and be set at different times. He also kept canaries in cages and the sound of the cuckooing clocks would set the canaries off chirruping and chirping. Next, the family parrot, Grumpy, would join in screaming and squawking, if he hadn't escaped that day. If he had escaped, he would often as not be sitting at the top of the tallest tree in their garden, waiting to be coaxed down.

To add to the din, Brownie the dog started barking as I went into the kitchen, where Prim's mum Ivy was preparing the evening meal. It was Friday and so, being good Catholics, they would be eating fish as usual. My mouth watered at the thought of the beautiful cod Ivy had served up the last time I was asked to stay and eat with the family. It had come with a beautiful parsley sauce and delicious creamed potatoes. I didn't mind missing out tonight, though. Every Friday night we always had fish and chips at home. Dad would get it from the shop opposite the Five Bells pub on the New Cross Road and we were allowed to eat it straight out of the paper.

'Hello Maureen, dear,' Ivy said, after telling Brownie to pipe down. 'How's your mum today?' Ivy was a lovely lady, always friendly. I could never understand how she could be married to Prim's dad.

'She's well, thank you,' I said.

Two of Prim's four older brothers burst into the kitchen. 'We're going out to feed the fish and the chickens,' said Arthur. 'Coming?'

We followed them out of the back door and past the outside toilet to the big chicken run, which was full of hungry, clucking hens. Reg carried the chicken feed out in a bucket. It was made with a combination of boiling water, potato peelings, leftover greens and something that looked like fine sand. It had a fabulous smell when it was all mixed up. You almost wanted to eat it yourself. I dipped my face into the bucket for a sniff. Beautiful. My mouth started watering again.

At the side of the house, there was a great big fish tank. It was at least six feet long and three feet wide. Inside were several enormous goldfish, as big as carp. The surface of the water broke and rippled as Arthur scattered fish food into the tank. I watched, fascinated, as their big-lipped mouths gaped open and shut.

'What shall we do?' Prim asked, when Reg and Arthur had gone back inside.

I shrugged. I was happy to tag along anywhere with Prim. She was tall, blonde, pretty and two years older than I was. I counted myself lucky that she was prepared to hang about with a nine-year-old like me at all.

I looked down to the end of her long garden. Just beyond the far wall there was a bombed building and a pepper factory. 'We could go up the bomb site?' I suggested. I was always going there with my friend Maureen Watts.

'We could,' Prim said, staring off into the distance. A gleam came into her eye. 'Or we could go and grab ourselves a couple of apples.'

My eyes widened. 'Yeah!' I said, laughing. 'Let's go scrumping!'

It would mean climbing over Prim's fence into Mr Ritchie's garden, at the risk of being caught and getting into trouble, but it was worth it. Mr Ritchie was a right old grump. Like Prim's dad, he frightened the kids in our street.

But he had these beautiful trees full of juicy apples and the thought of them was making my mouth water yet again. I was a constantly hungry child.

I looked at Prim. She gave me a wink. 'Come on!' she said, and we legged it over the fence and scaled up the nearest of Mr Ritchie's apple trees.

An hour later, I burst through the front door at home, gasping for breath.

'What have you been up to?' Mum asked me suspiciously.

I grinned. 'Nothing!'

'Come on, I know what you're like,' she said.

'We've been nicking Mr Ritchie's apples again,' I confessed.

'That's naughty!' she tutted, but there was a smile on her lips.

'Is it time for tea?' I asked. 'I'm starving!'

I was born – an eternally hungry little thing – on 1 August 1945, just before the end of the war. My mum nearly had me in Cardiff, where my dad was stationed, but two weeks before I arrived, he was transferred to Dorking in Surrey, and so that's where I was born. In a place like that, I should have come out speaking very posh! But there was no chance of that. Apparently, I was a terror from the word go, but even more so once I became a toddler.

'You was a cow,' my mum tells me. 'We'd be waiting at a bus stop and we'd look round to find you'd gone. "Where's Maureen? Where's Maureen?" we'd start yelling, in a panic.'

One day, she discovered me halfway down the road in one of those posh confectionery shops with frilly curtains in the windows and chocolates on display. According to the shop's owner, all that could be seen of me was this tiny hand delving into the window display, grabbing sweets and throwing the papers back.

'Whose little girl is this?' she said snootily. 'I don't mind her taking the chocolate, but to throw the papers back in the window is absolutely disgusting!'

'Come 'ere!' Mum shouted, mortified.

I was the type of kid who couldn't resist taking the middle orange out of an arrangement of fruit in a shop. Then the whole lot would fall down!

I was very strong-willed. One day, my mum and nan took me out with them to buy a gas iron, a big heavy thing. 'I want to hold it!' I insisted, threatening to create a scene if I didn't get my own way. Since I was quite a stocky kid, they let me carry it home. I marched along, swinging it as I went. The number of people I hit in the legs with that iron! 'Oi!' they winced, 'Watch it!' – all the way home.

I was two when my little sister Jackie was born. One afternoon, when Jackie was a fortnight old, Mum said to me, 'Come on, we're going up to bed to have a little sleep.'

She and the baby soon fell asleep, leaving me to my own devices. Well, it wasn't long before I'd found a box of matches and started striking them, one after another. Terrible, I was. A few minutes later, my mum rolled over to find the bed alight! Quick as anything, she picked up Jackie and me and ran downstairs, shouting to the bloke next door for help. He rushed into the house, opened all the windows, grabbed the burning mattress and managed to throw it out into the front garden. It didn't half give Mum a shock, but she saw the funny side afterwards – just about.

Mum says that I had at least five dummies and would

never let them go. I used to pop the rubber teats on my fingers and suck them each in turn. Then one day my granddad looked up and said, 'You keep sucking those dummies, you'll grow up looking like one.' With that, I took them off my fingers, threw them all on the fire and never used a dummy again.

I believed every word my mum's dad said. I was a terrible nail-biter and he warned me, 'You keep biting your nails, you'll blow up like a balloon.' That stuck in my head too.

Time went by and one day I was sitting on a bus opposite a pregnant woman. I stared and stared at her, until she said, 'Hello.' I just went on staring. 'Do you know me?' she asked, finally.

'No, but I know what you've been doing!' I blurted out. Mum didn't know where to look.

Oh God, I was terrible! When people asked me, 'What would you like to do when you grow up?' I'd say, 'I'd like to be a loose woman in Piccadilly!' I don't know where I got that from; I must have overheard it from someone. That was just the type of kid I was.

I was so saucy that Mum began to feel nervous when anyone spoke to me, for fear of what I'd say back. One of the worst instances was the day in 1947 we went to visit my dad, who was a chief petty officer and a boatswain in the Navy. On the train to Chatham, where he was docked, we sat opposite two old biddies. My mum had baby Jackie in her arms and me next to her.

'Hello, little girl,' said one of the old biddies. She pointed at Jackie. 'Is that your little brother?'

'No, that's my sister,' I said. 'She's got a minny. My dad's got a winkle and it's this big!' I held my hands wide apart to demonstrate. After that, whenever we were out and I went to say something, my mum would clap her hands over my mouth!

It wasn't just the things I said that got me into trouble, it was the things I did too. When I was five, my nan took me out one afternoon. While she was chatting with her friend outside some shops, I went off and came back with a pushchair. Nan didn't notice that it wasn't the one we'd come out with. 'All right, Ada, I'll see you later,' she said to her friend as she started pushing me home. It was only when we got back that she noticed a tag hanging off the frame. She had pushed me home in a brand new pushchair that I'd pinched from a shop! So of course she had to take it straight back.

I was always up to something. When I was six or seven and could read, I would see a shop sign saying, 'Please take one' or 'Please help yourself', and take whatever I fancied, without paying for it. I'd hide the goods in my doll's pram.

When we got home, my mum would go mad. 'I've got to take this back now!' she'd yell despairingly, putting her coat back on. There was no question of keeping anything that didn't belong to us. My mum and dad were strict in that way.

I was constantly getting told off. One time, while my mum was talking to a friend in a shop doorway, I spotted a window cleaner above us, busy cleaning windows. When no one was looking, I wheeled his ladder along the street, so that he couldn't get down. He was hopping mad when he realised what I'd done, and so was Mum.

'I need eyes in the back of my head to keep up with you, Maureen!' she used to moan. I was always Maureen then.

The family used to call me Mogsy sometimes, but never Mo. That came later.

New Cross in south-east London was a lovely place in the 1950s and there were plenty of shops in the high street, including two greengrocers, one on either side of the road, a fresh fish shop and an olde-worlde Boots the Chemist, done out in dark brown. Pipers on the corner sold Oxo, Bisto and tinned food, Harris's had all the bread, there was another baker's round the corner, a chicken shop, two cafés, a barber's, a craft shop, a knitting shop where you could buy all kinds of wool and a pet shop that sold raw meat for dog and cat food. There was also an oil shop, where you bought paraffin, wood and gas mantles. Most people still had gas lighting as well as electric.

All the shops had boards outside to advertise what they sold. When Mum wasn't looking, I'd swap them around. When I'd finished, the board outside the café said 'Household goods and pigeon feed', and the sign saying 'Tea, coffee and home-made cake' was outside the chandler's shop.

I vividly remember going shopping with my mum in the high street. The shops were always busy and I loved watching everybody go by. I often saw a couple who lived down in New Cross on the way to the Old Kent Road. I can remember as plain as daylight what they looked like. They were always smartly dressed: she carried a basket and wore a hairnet under her hat, a tweed coat, brown stockings and lace-up brown shoes; he was always in a black suit. They were both midgets.

There was a nice haberdasher's shop that Mum liked to go in. One day, while she was in there talking to the owner and the assistants were busy serving, me and my sister took all the boxes of shoes outside and lined them up along the pavement. That was another time I got into trouble, not to mention the time we fell asleep on the eiderdowns in the shop window.

My sister was entirely different to me and almost never misbehaved, unless she was with me. One of my favourite tricks was to lead her into Prim's chicken hutch and blindfold her. I'd line up bowls of different bits and pieces, like jam, marmalade and bread, then I'd feed them to her and she had to guess what they were. One time, I blindfolded her and swapped all the nice things for horrible stuff. 'Tell me what this is,' I said, spooning mustard into her mouth. Her screams could be heard from the end of the street!

Jackie and I had some terrible arguments. One day, while we were in the basement, she said something that annoyed me so much that I threw a sandwich at her. She ducked and the sandwich went flying over her head and splatted on the mirror on the wall behind her. That started a free-for-all and we flung every insult we could think of – and the rest of our sandwiches – at each other. Just then, Dad came home. He was furious when he came downstairs and saw the mess. I got a smack on the legs for that.

Even when we weren't arguing, me and Jackie used to get ourselves into trouble. We had a game that we played with a big green suitcase stored in the spare room upstairs. It was a smart, old-fashioned case with a brown leather handle, leather corner trim and a clip lock. One of us would get inside it and the other one would lock it and pull it around the room. We called it 'giving rides'.

'Come on, I'll give you a ride in the suitcase,' I said one day when Mum and Dad had gone out. It was OK for your parents to pop out for a couple of hours in those days.

Jackie jumped inside and I pulled her around the room for a while. Then it was my turn. I was bigger than she was and too big to fit easily inside the case, but I squashed myself in and eventually she managed to snap the locks shut, after a lot of huffing and puffing. Unfortunately, the case being too full put a strain on the locks; they jammed and I was trapped.

I was inside that case for about an hour, but it felt like hours and hours. Jackie was hysterical. 'I'll get it when Dad comes back!' she sobbed.

I was totally stiff and could barely breathe by the time Mum and Dad arrived home. It's a wonder I was still alive. Dad forced the case open and there I was, gasping for air. He was furious and clumped my sister right across the legs. Then he turned to me. 'What did you have to get in it for, in the first place?' he asked angrily, giving me a clump, too. 'You knew you was too big for it!' I've had a fear of closed-in spaces ever since.

Mum used to laugh at all my antics, but she was also quite protective. She wouldn't let me and Jackie have pushbikes. She said they were too dangerous, so we had to have scooters. She encouraged us to do tap dancing and ballet and we used to go for lessons at the local school hall every week. We'd dance about to the *Nutcracker* music, singing the words from the Stork margarine ad: *'Treat yourself to bread and magic!'* All the girls round our way did ballet or tap or ball-room dancing. Every year, the various dance schools in our area put on shows at Catford Town Hall.

Dad was definitely the stricter parent. I was more scared of him than I was of my mum, but he wasn't a bully and he never bashed us up, like some people's dads did. We never got hidings, just the occasional smack, and he'd sooner punish us by keeping us in, which was far worse than being clumped.

We had to be in at a certain time; we couldn't be late. If he said, 'I want you in by eight o'clock,' that was that. If you didn't come back in time, you were punished. 'You're in for a week!' he'd say. My heart would sink when I heard those words. I used to get so bored when I was grounded.

My best friend at the time was Maureen Watts, who lived in an upstairs flat in Billington Road, the street just behind ours. It was nice and cosy where she lived, all fitted carpet up the stairs, but I didn't go into her house a lot. I just used to knock on the door.

Maureen and I met at primary school, where we discovered on our first morning that we had been born on the same day. Physically, we were quite different: I was small and blonde with blue eyes; she had brown eyes and dark hair in a fringed bob. But we were very similar in personality, partners in crime. We used to play up a lot. We'd go up the bomb site and set up camps, or play 'Knock Down Ginger' down Billington Road. We had some good old times in our childhood. It was always fun. Two balls up the wall, skipping, pogo sticks – we were always busy doing something. Often we were joined by other kids on the street, including a little blond boy called Martin, who was almost as saucy as I was. Martin was one of five brothers and sisters. Maureen, Jackie and I were mates with all the kids in the family and his parents were friends with my parents. That's the way it was in those days – everyone knew everyone. We were a close-knit community.

If none of my mates were around, sometimes I'd knock on a neighbour's door and say, 'Can I take your baby out?' You could do that in those days, back when people didn't worry about leaving their kids outside shops in pushchairs and prams. You never heard about anyone getting murdered.

I'd enjoy it for a bit, saying 'Coo, coo' to the baby and watching it play with its rattle. But after walking up and down the street and round the block a few times, I'd get bored. When I was too fed up to go on, I'd nip the baby's fingers or give it a little pinch to make it cry, so I could take it back to the mum and say, 'The baby keeps crying. You'd better have him back.'

Some people might read that and think, blimey, what else did she do to them? But I wouldn't really hurt them! It was just to give me an excuse to take them home and go out on my own.

I didn't have many sweets as a child, but one of the highlights of the week was when the Corona lorry came round selling bottles of fizzy orange, grapefruit and blackcurrant pop. They were dirt cheap; there was a one penny deposit on each bottle and every week you'd hand the bottles back and get your next lot of pop. Another highlight was Saturday morning pictures at the local film theatre. Me and Jackie would go along to watch *Davy Crockett* or *20,000 Leagues Under the Sea* and throw things at the organist, along with 200 other kids.

My nan was the first in the family to have a telly. I loved *Muffin the Mule* and *Andy Pandy* as a kid. The ITV adverts were also pretty good. I can remember them all, from OMO and Tide Clean to Pepsodent and Camay. Back then, I was fascinated by crime stories. My favourite television programme was *Inner Sanctum Mystery*, which was on every Sunday. It was a mystery and suspense series full of murders and it really fired my imagination.

Every time we went away to my nan's or on a day trip and found ourselves on a platform, I'd watch wide-eyed as all the big trunks were loaded on the train. 'What's the matter, Maureen?' my mum would say.

'I think there's a dead body in that trunk over there!' I'd whisper, remembering the latest episode of *Inner Sanctum Mystery*.

'Honestly, Maureen, whatever will you say next?'

In those days I saw life as a big adventure, full of opportunities to have fun and make mischief. I was never really bad, just cheeky and inquisitive, but somehow those qualities combined always seemed to get me into trouble.

chapter two

Family Matters

MY MUM, KATHLEEN 'Kit' Cheriton, and my dad, Leonard Oldman, met during the war. They were both living in Cardiff at the time. Mum and her family had left London to escape the Blitz. She and her sister Renee worked in the Milk Bar in the centre of town, where all the British and American soldiers went. The bar was horseshoe-shaped, with the till in the middle. The Brits stayed on the left of the bar and the Yanks on the right.

Mum was dark-haired and elegant. She used to serve the British side. Renee, on the other hand, had long blonde hair and looked like Lauren Bacall, so naturally she served the Americans, who lavished her with stockings and chewing gum. Mum and Renee were always arguing about who was going to ring up at the till first. It was a source of constant irritation.

'I was here first!'

'You wasn't, I was. Anyway, it's my turn!' They never came to blows, but it was a close thing.

Fights occasionally broke out among the men. One evening, a soldier had a row with a little Welsh guy, who took his glass eye out and put it on the bar in case they traded punches. My mum was polishing the bar at that very moment and she swept the poor bloke's glass eye onto the floor. What a disaster. The fight was forgotten while everyone got down on their hands and knees to look for the little man's eye.

While Renee had her pick of the American soldiers, my mum didn't have much luck with boyfriends. She was too soft-hearted: she'd feel sorry for all the poor sods and go out with them out of pity.

One time she thought she'd caught a good one. 'He looks a very smart man!' remarked her mum about the latest bloke she'd started seeing.

Mum's new beau wore a dicky bow, clean cuffs and lovely, polished shoes. However, at the end of a week of courting her, he was still wearing exactly the same outfit as at the start of the week, and everyone had noticed that his dicky bow was false, as were the now grubby cuffs under his coat. Worse, his shiny shoes had holes in the soles and were lined with cardboard. So he got the thumbs down.

Eventually, my dad walked into the Milk Bar and that was that. Tall, handsome and blond, he spoke very nicely and looked lovely in his Navy outfit. Dad was working on a destroyer ship in Cardiff Docks. He was in charge of the rigging, anchors, hull maintenance and cables. I don't know if he saw action. He didn't talk about the war and never mentioned seeing dead people or killing anyone, so I think he was mainly stationed in one place.

He and my mum got married in 1944 and I came along the following year. There was Irish blood on Mum's side of the family, so they called me Maureen. My full name was Maureen Lesley Oldman. Meanwhile, Renee married a bloke called Arthur, who worked on the same ship as my dad. I don't know why she didn't go for a Yank in the end. Perhaps she had enough of a stockpile of chewing gum and stockings by then.

*

Before he joined the Navy, my dad worked with his father, Alf Oldman, who owned a painting and decorating business in New Cross, south-east London. When he left the Navy in 1947, Dad moved his little family back into Alf's house and took up the business again. We lived at 10 Hatcham Park Road, three doors down from Primrose's family and all their bizarre animals. Our house had three bedrooms upstairs and a front room, a middle room, a kitchen and scullery downstairs. Like Prim's house, it also had a big garden. We didn't have a bathroom; there was a tin bath that me and my sister used to share twice a week.

Granddad Alf was tall, with a moustache, and he always wore a cap. I don't know what happened to his wife, or whether he'd even had a wife, because she was never mentioned. When I was five, he fell ill and moved into the middle room downstairs. I vividly remember the day he died. Me and my sister were kept upstairs, but I peeped through the banister and saw my dad go into Granddad's room with a glass to put over his mouth to see if he was still breathing. He wasn't. There was a lot of fuss and crying after that, but I can't remember him being taken out of the house and we kids weren't allowed to go to the funeral.

A few days after Granddad died, we had a visit from his sister. 'Hello, Maud,' I heard my mum say in a sombre voice, showing an elderly lady into the front room. 'I'll call Leonard for you.'

While my sister and I waited upstairs, Maud dropped a bombshell in the front room. 'Alf wasn't your real father,' she told my dad, without mincing her words. 'He adopted you as a baby.' There was worse to come. 'It means that you won't be entitled to any share in the business,' she added primly. 'Sorry, but that's just the way it is.'

This came as a terrible shock to my dad. He had expected to inherit and suddenly he was left with nothing apart from Alf's rented house. I think it really affected him. Later, he found out that Alf was his father, after all. Apparently, Granddad had secretly had a fling with a young maid and she'd become pregnant. When she gave birth to my dad in 1921, Granddad took him in, adopted him legally and brought him up. There was no question of marrying the maid. She was never heard of again. I don't know why Granddad's sister didn't know the truth, but it was probably because the circumstances of Dad's birth had been swept under the carpet.

Anyway, nothing made any difference by then. The fact that Dad was illegitimate meant that his other relatives had a greater claim to his father's estate than he did, or so he was led to believe. I always had the impression that Dad had been done out of what was due to him. We never saw Maud or any of the rest of that side of the family again.

Until that day, my dad had hardly drunk a drop. Afterwards, he took to the drink more, but he was never a big drinker. He'd call into the pub for a couple of pints after a hard day's work, before he came home for his tea, and he might go to the pub on a Saturday or Sunday lunchtime. But I never saw him drink indoors and I only ever saw him drunk once, when he tripped and dropped the dinner and all the gravy on me and my sister one Christmas Day. Even then, he just seemed merry, because it was Christmas. He never stank of booze or swayed around like some people's dads.

After he stopped working for Granddad's business, he did a course to become a pipe fitter and welder and landed a job working for Matthew Hall Limited at Battersea Power Station, in south-west London. He used to get up every morning around five o'clock, have his breakfast and cycle to work. He went out at six in the morning and came home about five in the evening. He'd have a couple of pints, come in, have his tea, watch a bit of telly and go to bed.

He was a really nice dad, a tall, good-looking guy with a humorous twinkle in his eyes. I adored him. From the start, I was a daddy's girl. Throughout my childhood, I loved to do things for him. 'Come on, let's comb your hair,' I'd say, from when I was very small right up until I left home. We spent a lot of time together at weekends, up at the park, or making things at home. Sometimes he took me to see Millwall play on a Saturday. Dad was very athletic, a really good footballer and cricketer, and he'd been for a trial at Millwall when he was younger. He was also a great swimmer and had been the South London swimming and diving champion as a schoolboy.

When Dad came home from work, the kitchen would be filled with the delicious smell of my mum's home cooking. She was a proper housewife, my mum. She cleaned the house, washed our clothes, cooked our meals, met us from school, took us to tap-dancing classes around the corner and sat and knitted in the evenings. She was and still is a fabulous knitter.

On washing days, she used to boil up gallons of water in a great big copper pot. She washed our smalls by hand, using a wooden washboard, and then she wrung everything out through a mangle. I used to like turning the mangle wheel for her. She went to the launderette once a week to wash the bigger stuff and the sheets and collars were sent to be laundered. A van used to come and pick them up.

Mum was constantly cooking and we always had good, fresh food, not the new-fangled frozen stuff that was just catching on. I can't remember us ever going to a restaurant. I don't think there were many restaurants then, apart from tea houses. Takeaways were the new thing: Wimpy bars were the first to arrive and now and again you'd see a Chinese takeaway.

At home, Mum cooked liver and bacon, sausage, mash and onions, toad in the hole, minced meat, stuffed marrows, roly polys and steak and kidney puddings steamed in cloth. One of our favourite dishes was tripe and onions cooked in milk, with mashed potatoes. Dad made us laugh by calling it 'stewed knitting' because of the way it looked. Puddings were usually a delicious concoction of sponge and syrup, or stewed apples and custard. We didn't have anything like the variety of fruit that there is now. There were apples and oranges, but I didn't see fruit like grapes or pineapples until I was older.

Mum was very happy-go-lucky, always singing and dancing. 'Danny Boy' and 'Mother Of Mine' were two of her favourite songs and I often heard her humming 'Can't Help Lovin' Dat Man', 'My Yiddishe Momme' and the Andrews Sisters song 'Bei Mir Bist Du Schön (Means That You're Grand)'. When we had a long walk ahead of us, she'd say, 'How many songs do you think we can get through before we're there?' We often had singalongs around my nan's piano. My mum and nan could both play well and Mum and her sister used to harmonise, like the Kaye Sisters.

Mum made everything fun. A placid type of person, she never rowed with people, never got involved in arguments or took sides, never hollered and hooted or even raised her voice. She never told tales or gossiped, either. As a result, all the neighbours liked her. Now and again, Mum and Prim's mum Ivy would get together to study the horses and have a little flutter. They'd look through the paper and put down a sixpenny or a shilling bet on the horse they favoured that day. They loved having a flutter.

Dad didn't earn much, but we never went without. We weren't poor, although we didn't have a lot of money; I suppose you could say we were on the border of being middle class, without actually being middle class. Dad and Mum always seemed very happy together and they were very loving parents. Looking back, I'd say we were a really happy family. There was a lot of love in our house and Jackie and I never went without cuddles. We were lucky.

Like me, Mum was the eldest child, but in her case, she was one of three sisters: Renee was the middle daughter and the youngest girl was Shirley, ten years younger than my mum. Born in Sutton in 1919, Mum was very clever. She could already read and write by the time she went to school, so they sent her home, because there was nothing to teach her.

Her mother, my nan Victoria, could read teacups. People said she was psychic and she certainly had some kind of gift of knowledge. One day, she was in the middle of ironing when she said to my mum, 'Come on, Kit, get your coat on. We've got to go now!' She put the iron to cool and they left the house.

They went to the bus stop, but when the bus came along Nan's feet wouldn't leave the ground. It was as if they were glued to the pavement. 'Come on, Mum,' Kit said. 'If we're going, let's get on the bus.'

'No, we're on the wrong side of the road,' said my nan suddenly. 'We should be on the other side of the road, going the other way.'

So they crossed the road and got on another bus. 'Where exactly are we going?' Kit asked.

'I'll tell you when we get there,' said my nan.

As they pulled up in front of Morden Station, my nan had a feeling. 'It's time to get off,' she said.

There was a café next to the station. Plain as day, through the café window, they saw my granddad sitting at a table with the woman he was having an affair with. My nan had caught him red handed, by following her sixth sense. She clumped him so hard she broke her arm, even though he denied doing anything untoward.

'But I caught you with her!' she said.

'You must have dreamed it,' he said. 'It was all in your imagination.'

That was the only time he ever strayed, I think. They always seemed quite happy and harmonious whenever I was with them.

We weren't allowed to call mum's father Granddad; it had to be 'Uncle Bill', because he didn't want to feel old. Bill was always immaculately turned out in a pin-striped suit with a carnation or a rose in his lapel. He wore a smart navy blue hat. His day job was driving articulated lorries for Pickfords, moving theatrical sets all over the country for various theatre and entertainment companies. In his spare time, he was a bit of an impresario. He hired a hall over in Rosehill in Morden, set up his own theatre and put on variety shows, signing up amateur singers, dancers and stand-ups to do turns.

Along the way, he discovered a stand-up joke teller whose

stage name was Ernie Mason. After my granddad auditioned him and gave him a regular slot in his shows, a talent spotter from the BBC came along and picked him out for a radio audition. Not long afterwards, Ernie Mason changed his name, first to Duke Daly and then to Charlie Chester. The rest is history, as he went on to become the nation's favourite comic broadcaster during and after the war. My granddad was always proud of the part he played in Charlie Chester's rise.

I was very close to my nan and granddad. We often went to stay with them in Sutton during my childhood and Nan regularly came to stay at our house with Shirley, who was more like a sister than an aunt. Young, attractive and glamorous, she looked a bit like Princess Margaret and used to drive articulated lorries. She could drive anything, even tractors. We didn't see much of Renee, Mum's other sister, because by then she was living in Mottingham, over Bromley way, with her husband and children.

In 1953, my dad went out to the West Indies to work on the bauxite plants near Mandeville in Jamaica. He was away for a year, but the time flew past. He was back before we knew it. Then he decided to go back to Mandeville again in 1955. The work was well paid and he liked the lifestyle. The only downside was being away from his family.

'What's it like there?' I asked him, before he left. I didn't want him to go. I much preferred it when he was at home.

His face broke into a grin. 'Maybe you'll have a chance to find out for yourself, if you're a good girl,' he said.

My heart leapt. 'You mean, we could come and visit you?'

'Only if you behave yourself while I'm away.'

'I will, I promise!' I said excitedly.

About six months before we were due to go and join Dad, Mum packed up the house, sublet it to a newly married couple and we went to live at my nan's in Sutton. Uncle Billy had died the year before, so Nan was glad of the company. We all missed my granddad, but obviously his death hit my mum and nan harder than it hit me or Jackie. As a child you just get on with things, without giving them too much thought.

Nan lived in a red brick two-bedroom house with a green front door and red ochre steps leading up to it. It was very homely and comfortable inside, with fitted carpets, a piano, a television and a big radiogram. Every week, we polished the brass letterbox and knocker with Brasso.

I slept in with Nan, and Mum and Jackie slept together. The bedrooms had big comfortable beds with lovely eider-downs and soft pillows. Me and Jackie went to school in Sutton and Mum got a job as an usherette in the local picture palace. She did it for something to do, to give my nan the keep and earn a bit of pocket money on the side.

I had vowed to Dad that I would be good, but I couldn't stick to my promise. I had to entertain myself, after all, and inevitably I got into trouble. One afternoon, I was playing in a field next to the Sutton bypass with a kid called Bobby. It was a boiling hot summer and we were sodding about with some matches. All of a sudden, the grass caught alight. We had to run for it, because the whole field along the bypass shot up in flames. Hundreds of rats swarmed out, sped across the road and ran through people's gardens and sheds. My nan's shed was swarming with them.

When I got home, Nan was on the phone. 'Nan! The field's alight!' I said breathlessly. 'Can you call the fire engines?'

'What happened?' she asked.

'I don't know,' I lied. 'We was just coming home and saw the field burning!'

Twenty fire engines arrived to battle the flames. I went out to watch them, feeling ever so guilty, but at least it never got back to my dad. Luckily for me, he was none the wiser that I hadn't strictly kept my promise.

chapter three

Amazing Adventures

W E SET SAIL for Jamaica in late February 1956. I was ten years old and could barely contain my excitement. Not only was I going on the biggest adventure of my life, but while we were away I would miss taking my eleven plus exams. The timing could not have been better!

We went by boat because it was cheaper than flying. The fare was eighty quid, all in. It took three weeks going and two weeks coming back. Our ship, the SS *Covina*, was a big banana boat filled with general cargo for the outward journey and bananas on the way back, with room for a few hundred passengers as well. We travelled second class, which meant we weren't stuck down in the bottom of the ship, but we weren't at the top, either!

Me and my sister had a ball. Being kids, we got up to mischief all day, along with a boy called Graham who was about our age and just as naughty. We ran amok, trying to get into forbidden parts of the boat like the engine room, sneaking into the lifeboats, trying to nick food from the kitchens and making up stories about the passengers. Once a week there was an emergency drill, in case we sank. Me, Jackie and Graham enjoyed the drill. It made the trip seem even more exciting.

When we weren't up to mischief, we played deck quoits and went swimming in the pool. We often saw flying fish and once when we were staring over the deck rail out to sea, we saw a pod of dolphins swimming along and leaping out of the water. It was wonderful.

A gong sounded for breakfast, lunch and dinner, which I loved, although there were only a few kids on board and we had different meal times to the adults. There wasn't much for us to do in the evenings. We used to stay in our cabin and play I-Spy, Two Balls, Jack Five and skipping. There were dances and bingo for the adults, so it was a lot better for them.

Everyone got dressed for dinner and some people really went to town with their outfits. My mother used to tell us about one particular woman who owned a selection of beautiful dresses. I didn't see her because she was travelling in first class, but she was very la-di-dah, apparently.

One evening, Mum came back from dinner chuckling. 'What happened?' I asked her.

'Well,' she said, dissolving into giggles, 'I shouldn't laugh...' – although she was so tickled pink that she could hardly get the words out.

It turned out that the la-di-dah woman had been on the captain's table that night wearing a beautiful sequinned dress with spaghetti straps. My mum was on a table nearby, so she had a very good view of her.

While the main course was being served, the woman dropped her napkin on the floor and, as she bent down to pick it up, the bodice of her dress fell down, revealing her naked breasts. A steward was standing nearby, dishing up vegetables with a big silver spoon. He was obviously so shocked by the sight of this woman's bare breasts that in a moment of madness he went to help her back into her dress with the spoon he was holding! Oh, the horror of it! The woman fled the dining room and no one saw her again for the rest of the journey. She had all her meals in her cabin.

It was quite a journey. We had to cross the Bay of Biscay, which is famous for its rough seas and fierce storms. For most of the crossing, huge waves crashed over the top deck and the boat listed heavily from one side to the other. Me and Jackie sat on the stairs down below, hanging on for dear life. The staircase kept swinging from vertical to horizontal and back again, and all around us, people were falling over and getting injured. We loved it! It was so exciting. Being kids, we had no fear, but the adults must have been seriously worried about sinking.

It was definitely an eventful trip. One day, someone dived into the pool when it was empty and broke his neck. The ship's doctor was always drunk, and when we stopped at Barbados and Trinidad, quite a few of the crew didn't come back. Barbados was our first taste of the Caribbean, a green jewel in a blue diamond sea. My strongest memory of the island is of seeing the most incredible shop window display in a little town near the docks. Me and Jackie couldn't believe our eyes: to celebrate Easter, the whole window was full of little live chicks. There must have been a couple of hundred of them and they were all dyed different colours. There were pink, yellow, orange, black, lavender and tangerine chicks toddling around and pecking corn. It was a fantastic sight, absolutely beautiful. We stared and stared, totally enchanted. Mum had to drag us away when it was time to get back on the ship.

Our next stop was Trinidad, which was every bit as beautiful as Barbados. I remember picking leaves from all the different bushes and trees we came across. One of the other passengers showed us how to crush them and rub them in our hands to produce a whole range of interesting smells, from lime to tamarind. We saw strange insects on the ground and multi-coloured birds in the sky, including all kinds of tiny hummingbirds. Everything amazed us. It felt like we were entering a magical world of new sights and sounds.

Four days later, we reached Jamaica. We arrived in the evening and had to dock outside the port because of the tides, before we went in for disembarkation the next day. I'll never forget my first view of Kingston. It was lit up like a Christmas tree, with rows and rows of little lights twinkling away in the darkness. I had never seen anything so stunning. It took my breath away to see it from the ship's deck.

The heat was intense; it was boiling hot. All the cabin windows were open. 'Cor, isn't it hot, Mum?'

'Yeah,' was all my mum could say, using her energy to fan her face with a piece of paper.

Jamaica immediately felt different to Barbados and Trinidad. The dockside was so much busier; it was teeming with people dressed in colourful clothes, selling anything from beads to coconuts. There was a steel band playing rhythms I'd never heard before and all kinds of unfamiliar smells hit my nostrils. I was in awe of it all.

I got off the boat carrying a black doll with astrakhan hair, which was a bit like tight poodle hair. I don't know why I had that doll with me, because I wasn't really a doll person; I was always more of a tomboy. It came from Gamages department store at Holborn Circus and I think it was a Christmas present. With my child's logic, I must have taken it with me because I was going to a place where black people lived.

My dad picked us up from the port. As he met us at Customs, he noticed the doll in my hand. 'You can't have that here! Put it away and don't get it out again!' he said, looking flustered. He didn't give a reason. I put it in my suitcase and left it there.

Once we were through Customs, we bundled into the great big American station wagon Dad was driving. It was a Cadillac, I think, a beautiful car. I'd never seen anything like it in London, only in Hollywood films. It was a long way to Christiana-Spaldings, where we were staying. The roads twisted and turned as we rose up into the hills. 'Here we are,' Dad said, as we turned into a long driveway lined with pink and purple bougainvillea. Me and Jackie craned our necks to see out front. Suddenly the Villa Bella Hotel came into view, a long two-storey building with a tiled roof, its bright white exterior set off by the startling blue sky. This was to be our home for the next seven months.

I can picture it perfectly, even today. High on a hill, the hotel had a massive outside verandah, with an amazing view of the countryside, and a large adjoining lounge. The bedrooms were all on the other side of the building. I shared a bedroom with my sister. Our room was lovely, with a balcony overlooking the hills, but at first we were more concerned with the creepy crawlies on the floor. There were geckos and lizards, maybugs, tarantulas, huge cockroaches, moths and little red and black insects. We stood on chairs for the first week, petrified! That didn't last long. Two weeks down the line, we'd pick up the insects and race them, and it wasn't long before we had pet lizards.

The Villa Bella was owned by two white Jamaican sisters, Maria and Ida. Maria was the younger one and she had jet-black hair. Ida was the eldest; she was a big lady, taller than Maria, with grey hair. Ida always wore a dark house coat to cover her clothes. I don't remember seeing her wearing anything else in all the time we were there.

A lot of the guests either lived permanently in the hotel or they worked with my dad at the bauxite plant and were staying for a few months. At the plant, my dad had an apprentice called Danny Ashman, who was only seventeen at the time. Danny went on to have a daughter, Frances, who I met up with again nearly forty years later, purely coincidentally, in amazing circumstances. More of that later.

We had our breakfast, lunch, afternoon tea and evening meal in an airy dining hall on the ground floor. There were about nine or ten tables, each with a white tablecloth. The windows went from floor to ceiling, so the view was amazing and we'd eat looking out over the mountains and the banana plantations. The breakfast table was always heaving with fresh fruit, with juicy mango and pineapple, guavas, breadfruit and otaheite apples. My sister was a bit wary about trying all this new food, but I loved it. After stocking up on fruit, cornflakes, toast and eggs, I'd say excitedly, 'What can we do today, Jack?'

I loved my days. We had a wonderful time. I often spent my mornings around the back of the hotel with the maids and the 'boys', as they called the male staff, having a nose around to see what they were cooking and what I could pinch to eat. I still love Caribbean food today, especially curried goat, jerk chicken and yams.

Me and Jackie made friends with all the other kids in and around the hotel. We ran wild through people's gardens, dodging the owners and playing games. We played tennis, tried to dig up the poisonous frogs on the lawns and petted the cows, sheep and chickens that roamed in the fields nearby. We tried fruit we'd never even heard of and drank water from the tap, strictly against our parents' advice. Occasionally, the heavens would open and we'd get soaked and hole up in people's houses. Everything was exciting and interesting. It was another world. We never went to school – that might have been part of the enjoyment, I suppose! We just played for seven months. It was one long endless holiday, and we'd never really been on holiday before. We'd been for day trips to Hastings and Southend, Bognor and Brighton, but that was as far as my horizons had stretched until now.

The Jamaican kids we met couldn't understand our cockney accents, so we began to speak slower and more clearly. 'Hell-o! What is your name? My name is Maureen and this is my sister, Jacqueline,' I enunciated. Before long, we were talking proper English!

Before I went to Jamaica, I had never met a black person before. No black people went to our school in New Cross, so we hadn't really even seen any, apart from in films or on television. Nevertheless, it didn't feel like a big deal to me. I had no sense of there being any racism; I wasn't that way inclined, anyway, and it wasn't the way I was brought up.

Jamaica was very different then to how it is now. Everybody we met was proper old school, very friendly and smart. The men wore zoot suits and big hats. The women wore white gloves. People were very polite. They called my mum 'Mrs Len' and my dad 'Mr Len'. Everyone seemed nice.

Mum spent her days reading books and she did a lot of embroidery, a skill she had learned as a young girl. Dad came home every night and we saw him at weekends as well, if he didn't have to work. Sometimes he would take us out of an evening round to friends' houses, or we'd be invited to lunch somewhere on a Sunday. Wherever we went, we always seemed to be laughing.

If we stayed at the hotel, me and Jackie would sometimes sing and dance a bit in the evenings to entertain the other guests. At weekends we often went down to Montego Bay to swim with Mum and Dad, go to a restaurant or take a trip in a glass-bottomed boat and look at all the fish. Or we'd go to the Tropicana Club, or an open-air picture palace to watch a film. Children were welcome everywhere. It wasn't like England, where you couldn't go in pubs until you were eighteen.

It was a completely different way of life and I loved it. I can shut my eyes and go straight back there. It's one of those experiences that stays in your mind. Jamaica was such a contrast to England in so many ways. It wasn't just the beautiful countryside and the tropical weather – there were so many things I'd never seen before except in films, like showers and bidets and great big lift-up deep freezers, gorgeous leather Chesterfield suites and huge Yankee cars, like the Cadillac Dad drove. London had nothing like it, as far as I knew. We even had our clothes made for us while we were there.

Towards the end of our stay, me and Jackie were invited to present a bouquet of flowers to Sir Hugh Foot, an important British diplomat who was in Jamaica to visit the Prime Minister, Alexander Bustamante, and discuss Jamaica's move to independence, which finally happened in 1962. Sir Hugh was out there with his wife and as I handed him my bouquet, I said, 'Here's a bunch of flowers for you.'

'Thank you kindly,' he said with a smile.

'Sorry we ain't got one for your Lady's Foot,' I added cheekily. I always played up; I couldn't help myself.

When it came time to come home, Dad took us back to the docks. There were bananas everywhere; every surface of the dock seemed yellow. I watched the men loading them onto the SS *Covina*, strapping them into great big bundles and hauling them up the ramps. It was an amazing sight.

I was very sad to leave Jamaica when we sailed back home in October 1956, and upset to hear that the SS *Covina* was scrapped after the journey. We'd really had a lovely stay and met so many friendly people. It was one big happy time. When we got back to London, everyone laughed about how posh me and Jackie were speaking. We didn't think we were; we were just used to speaking clearly and pronouncing all our syllables. Me, Mum and Jackie were all a nice colour and our tans took ages to go. That was another novelty, because people didn't lie out in the sun to get a tan like they do now.

As our colour faded, our posh accents disappeared and six months down the line we were back into the cockney lingo again! I went back to school, the Christopher Marlowe all-girls secondary school in New Cross. I quite liked it there. I was good at art and I liked sports. I liked anything to do with drawing and making things. I wasn't bad at cooking and needlework and although I didn't like history and geography, I was quite good at making maps. I was no good at English or arithmetic, though. I couldn't get to grips with them. I only liked things that interested me; other than that, I never listened.

One thing I was very good at was doing impressions, which didn't get me anywhere at school, obviously, but it was a good party trick. People were always asking me to do my latest impression. I don't know where this particular talent came from – I'd just watch people and copy them: Ruby Murray, Alma Cogan, James Stewart in *Rear Window*, Connie Francis, Paul Anka, Johnny Rae and Frankie Lymon and the Teenagers. I went to the pictures as often as I could and listened to the radio nonstop. I was crazy about Frankie Lymon and the first record I ever bought, when I was twelve, was 'I'm Not A Juvenile Delinquent'.

The summer after we got back from Jamaica, we went on our first family holiday to Butlins at Clacton. We drove there, because by then Dad had a car, an Austin with a running board and indicators that came out on arms. There weren't a lot of cars around then, so we felt really lucky. There were only one or two cars parked on each street in our area.

Everybody came to Butlins: my dad, my mum, my nan, my mum's sister Shirley and me and Jackie. We were down there for a week and it was a lot of fun. There were donkey rides on the beach and bicycle rides along the front. We competed in egg and spoon races and the three-legged race. Dad did archery. We all went swimming in the pool and boating on the pond. Me and Jackie ate our weight in candyfloss, shrimp and winkles.

On the last night of the holiday, I entered the talent competition and did a few of my impressions. I only did it for a laugh, so no one was more surprised than I was when I won a silver cup and a free week's family holiday back at Butlins in September, for me, my mum, dad and sister!

Amid all the excitement, a woman came up to me and asked if I'd like to audition for a pantomime at the Finsbury

Park Empire that coming Christmas. It was a production of *Cinderella* starring the comedian Danny La Rue and a comic and singer called Dave King, who went on to be a film actor. Danny La Rue was absolutely stunning in those days: tall and slim with jet black hair. He was set to play one of the ugly sisters – the good-looking one – and the actor and playwright Alan Haines was playing the other sister. Dave King would be Buttons. It was a stellar cast, as they say.

The audition was held in a hall opposite Madame Tussauds at Baker Street. I did a bit of tap dancing, sang a couple of songs by Alma Cogan and Connie Francis, and was picked to join a little troupe called Eleanor Beam's Breezy Babes, who would form the chorus in the pantomime. I was small for my age – my sister had long outgrown me – and I was the second smallest kid in the group. We rehearsed every week in a little hall in Clapham. There was a lot to learn, because we had three separate segments to perform: we had to sing and dance to the Bing Crosby song 'Busy Doing Nothing' and we also had a ballet routine and a tap routine.

It was an exciting time. I loved the atmosphere of the theatre, all the lights behind the stage, the curtains and ropes and pulleys. The countdown to going on stage was exhilarating. I loved going into the make-up room to have my face daubed with stage paint and get changed into my different costumes. I was very nervous on the first night, though. 'Don't forget none of the steps!' I kept telling myself. It's quite hard to sing and dance at the same time and at one point we had to dance around these little seats, then sit down on them, cross our legs and raise them in the air.

God, I hope I don't fall over, I thought.

I must have done all right, because my mum and nan were beaming at me when I came off stage. 'You're a natural!' Nan said. 'Your granddad would have been so proud of you if he'd been here today.' We all felt sad that he hadn't lived to see me on stage at the Finsbury Park Empire, because he had devoted so much of his time to the world of theatre and performers.

One night, the unthinkable happened and I tripped up in the middle of a dance. I was mortified at first, but the audience fell about and I realised that I could get lots of laughs if I sodded around. I loved hearing the roar of the crowd if I missed a step or stepped out of the line and, as time went on and my confidence grew, I started to do my own thing on stage. *'Busy doing nothing,'* I'd sing, dancing off in the wrong direction, accidentally on purpose.

Unfortunately, this didn't go down well with Dave King, a.k.a. Buttons. He really got the hump with me. One night, after the audience had howled and clapped me for muddling everything up, he grabbed me by the plaits and yanked me towards him. 'Just stick to singing!' he hissed. 'I'm the one who gets the laughs, not you!' After that, he always gave me horrible looks before we went on stage, as if to say, 'You behave yourself out there.' I hated him for it. I was only having a bit of fun, after all.

The run lasted six weeks and overlapped with my school term, so we had a teacher in to give us lessons to make up for it. I didn't take much notice of him. I was a bit of a tearaway, always being told off because I didn't pay attention. After the pantomime was done, it didn't occur to me to audition for any other productions, or keep in touch with the director or anything. I could have followed it up and built on my experience but I didn't. That was it, as far as I was concerned. I went back to my tap and ballet classes in New Cross and carried on singing for fun. I never thought any more of it.

There was something else to focus on, anyway. Mum had been feeling ill and faint for months by the time the pantomime finished. She couldn't understand what was wrong with her, but she kept plodding on, until her sister Shirley said, 'Why don't you go down the doctor's and have a check-up?'

'Yeah, I s'pose so,' Mum said.

So she went to the doctor and explained that she hadn't been feeling well for months. Imagine her shock when she found out she was six months pregnant! 'But I haven't put on any weight or had any of the usual symptoms!' she protested, when the doctor broke the news. Her clothes fitted her right up to the last minute. Even when she was nine months pregnant, she was still wearing her usual skirts, only with a safety pin holding the buttonhole together.

When she worked out the dates, she realised that she must have conceived during our first family holiday at Butlins. 'I don't know how comes I got pregnant!' she said later, because she and my dad used Rendells suppositories, which contained a spermicide. The spermicide powder had come off them, though, and that's how it must have happened. Poor Mum, I don't think she wanted any more children, aged nearly forty. She'd had me at twenty-six and Jackie at twenty-eight – and now another baby, more than a decade later!

My baby brother Gary was born on Friday 21 March 1958, when I was twelve and a half. Mum had him at home. I remember Dad telling me and Jackie, 'Your mum's in labour, so stay out of the way, keep yourself occupied and try not to make too much noise.'

We were in the kitchen when the midwife arrived. Dad showed her upstairs, so we didn't even catch a glimpse of her. We could hear all this moaning and groaning coming from upstairs, but we weren't worried. We were kids and it never occurred to us that Mum could be in danger. Anyway, Dad didn't seem too concerned when he came down to fetch hot water.

The next thing I remember was Dad saying, 'You've got a little brother!' He was beaming with happiness.

Me and Jackie were thrilled. Once they'd cleaned him up, we went up there to see him. He was a tiny thing, only about four and a half pounds, and he was lovely. Everyone doted on him. A baby boy! Our happy family felt complete.

chapter four

Still So Young

GARY WAS A good kid. I don't remember him crying a lot. Me and Jackie spoilt him. Everyone spoilt him; he didn't want for anything. Mum loved him to bits. Dad bought him a train set and a Scalextric set, Action Men and skateboards. He was the apple of everybody's eye.

Me and Jackie had a lot of fun with baby Gary. We constantly cuddled him when he was a baby and we played with him as he grew up. We used to dress him up for fun, as an Arab or a cowboy. We thought it was hilarious to see him toddling about with a little cowboy hat on, waving his toy guns around.

When he started talking I used to take him to the local coffee bar, the Sombrero, and bribe him to swear in front of everybody.

'But I don't want to swear!' he'd whimper.

'I'll give you half a crown,' I'd say.

'All right,' he'd finally agree.

'Now then, tell everyone what cowboys have,' I'd say.

He'd change his mind again. 'I don't want to!'

'Look, I've got half a crown here,' I'd remind him, showing him the coin in my hand. 'What have cowboys got?'

'Big bollocks,' he'd whisper, barely audibly, causing a huge outbreak of laughter in the café.

I had never stopped playing up, and now I started hopping the wagon with Maureen Watts and missing school. I wasn't clever like my mum. I've never been clever. I didn't read books as a youngster and I had no interest in learning what they taught us at school. When I did turn up, I messed about. I was constantly being told off for not listening in class. Then I was caught cheating in a test: I had the answers written on my petticoat underneath my drill slip!

The teacher sent me straight home. 'You won't be taking any exams,' she said severely. She was right, I didn't.

My dad was furious when he got the letter saying what I'd done. 'That's it. You're in again!' he said. I wasn't allowed out for a fortnight.

I left school at fifteen, without any qualifications or career ambitions. Like most of the girls I knew, I was expecting to follow in my mother's footsteps and get married and be a housewife. In the meantime, I spent all my pocket money on Chubby Checker and Frankie Lymon records and started going to coffee shops with my mate Jennifer Crew, who lived round the corner in Erlanger Road. We progressed from youth clubs to moody little places where older kids met up to play music and dance. There were little clubs here, there and everywhere in London. We also went to see every single Elvis Presley film that was released. Everyone loved Elvis.

I hit adolescence around fifteen, just before I left school. I was still a bit of a tomboy. All I wanted to wear was my drainpipe jeans and baseball boots. My dad hated seeing me in my jeans, so when I went out with my mates, I'd leave the house carrying a handbag and wearing a skirt and blouse. The first chance I had, I'd change into jeans and boots, then I'd change back into the skirt before I went home.

Me and Jennifer used to want to stay out late, but I had to be in by eleven o'clock. My dad was strict. 'What do you want to do after eleven o'clock at night?' he'd ask suspiciously. We didn't do anything much; we'd just be round someone's house drinking Babychams or light ales. We didn't smoke or go in pubs, none of us did.

In order to stay out later, Jennifer used to tell her mum she was staying round my house and I'd tell my mum that I was staying round her house. Then, in the early hours, we'd walk back to my house and sneak in through the basement, where my sister's bedroom was. Still wearing my drainpipes, I'd lower myself into the basement eyrie and knock on her window. 'Jackie! Open the door!'

'But Dad—!' she'd say when she saw me and Jennifer.

'Don't you dare tell him what time I got in!' I'd say. We'd stay in her room until Dad went to work in the morning, when Jennifer went home and I crept upstairs to my room. This went on for months and months and we didn't get caught, partly because Jennifer's family didn't have a phone.

Then one day Jennifer's mum and my mum met in the street. 'Thanks for having Maureen,' my mum said.

'What do you mean? I was going to thank you for having Jennifer!' her mum said.

'Please don't tell Dad!' I begged Mum, when she confronted me later that day.

'All right,' she said, looking worried. 'But you've got to stop this now, you hear me? Your dad is bound to catch you out eventually.'

Mum was very soft with us, very lovey-dovey. When I got into trouble, she'd say, 'Oh dear, perhaps you shouldn't have done that.'

We could wind her around our fingers. 'Go on, Mum, let me go out! Don't let Dad know.'

'All right, but make sure you get back before he gets home from work, and don't let on I've said anything.'

Two weeks after I left school, I landed my first job, in the laboratory at Johnson's Cables. I was paid £2 13s a week for doing basic office work and I gave it all to my mum. It wasn't a lot. By the time she'd given me my fares to go to work, there wasn't much left. I wasn't at Johnson's Cables long, a couple of months, maybe. Then I got bored and left, because there wasn't enough to do and I needed to keep busy.

Next I started work in Boots the Chemist on the New Cross Road, round the corner from our house. I quite liked the work. It could get boring at times, but I enjoyed dealing with the public and there were a few funny moments. The pharmacist was Scottish, a nice man. The other assistant was a kindly older lady. The manager, on the other hand, was a grumpy old git. I didn't like him at all. He had greased-back hair, smelled of pipe tobacco and wore a black pin-striped suit that was shiny with wear and needed a good clean. He was very strict and constantly told me off. 'Maureen! Why haven't you cleaned this shelf, like I told you to?'

Most of the stock was kept behind the counter in drawers, on shelves and in the back room. There was one big old-fashioned till that me and the older assistant shared. Whenever a man came sidling in, looking sheepish, I'd say loudly, 'Can I help you, sir?' I always knew what he was after. I was aware of the facts of life, after all. Not that I'd ever done it, but I knew what was what.

Inevitably, he'd shoot away in the opposite direction and start studying a display box at the other end of the counter.

I was only little and looked young for my age, so he didn't want anything to do with me. Instead, he'd hang around either for the older assistant or the manager to be free. In the meantime, I'd say, 'What is it you want, then?' Finally, the poor bloke would catch the other assistant's eye and murmur his requirements to her, and she'd fetch him a packet of condoms.

I left Boots after a few months, because I just couldn't get on with the manager. I did all kinds of jobs during the next couple of years, from working in the print with Maureen Watts at Unilever Brothers to helping out in a butcher's near Regent's Park and packing boxes at a Peek Freans biscuit factory. Sometimes I only did a day here or a week there: stacking shelves; working as a petrol pump attendant; serving behind the bar of a pub; putting drainpipes together in a factory. I did everything. My mum used to come to all my job interviews with me, because I hated going on my own. I wanted my mum to be there for me and wait for me until I came out!

Every time I left a job, I'd look in the paper the next day and underline anything I thought I could do, then ring them up and ask for an interview. Sometimes I'd go after a job and they'd say, 'Really, we want someone with experience.'

'But if you don't get a chance to try it, how can you ever become experienced?' I'd say. 'You have to start somewhere.'

'Oh well, you know...' they'd mutter, never answering the question.

'I think you owe me my fare, then,' I'd say indignantly. 'Because you should have told me before I arrived that you wanted someone with experience. You've got me here on false pretences. I wouldn't have turned up if I'd known.'

Why hadn't they said on the phone that they only wanted someone experienced? Sometimes I'd travel halfway across London for an interview, so it was only right to ask for my fare back. Mostly, it would only be half a crown, but it all added up.

When I did get a job, it usually didn't last long. I was too restless, too eager to move on to something more challenging. I didn't mind working, but I needed something more fulfilling to do, although I was unlikely to find it with no qualifications and limited experience. Still, at least I was getting paid – when I was working, that is.

When I was about sixteen, I'd make myself up to look a bit older and go along to the Five Bells on a Friday night with my dad, mum and Mum's sister Shirley. It was a lively place on Fridays: there was someone on the piano, someone else on the drums and a lot of people got up and did a turn. Mum used to get up and sing Kaye Sisters songs with her sister and occasionally I'd muster the courage to sing 'Walking My Baby Back Home' or something by Ruby Murray, Alma Cogan or Connie Francis.

I was always up to something as a kid and didn't give a sod, but I think I became more self-conscious as I got older. I had to be pushed when someone said, 'Go on, get up and sing!'

'No, no!' I'd say, because I didn't think I was any good. Some people say I've got a good voice, but I can't see it. I certainly wasn't one of these people who says, 'I'll get up and do a song!' Once I started to sing, it was all right. It was the getting up and doing it that was hard.

Mostly I went out with Jennifer, though. Maureen Watts had moved away by then. Me and Jennifer were always trying to find somewhere to dance; all we were interested in was rock and roll and we soon started going to dance clubs. We were good dancers; we knew we were good, because people used to stop and watch us. Jennifer was pretty with short dark hair; she was much taller than me, so when we danced, she led and I twirled around her. On Saturdays, we went to the Co-op Dance Hall or the Tottenham Royal. On Sunday afternoons we'd head for the Lyceum Ballroom in the West End.

On a Sunday, Jennifer would come round to my house and we'd get ready together. I'd backcomb my hair, lacquer it until it was stiff and put it up in a bouffant beehive, or a pleat. I'd rub pan stick on my face – and on my lips, to give me a ghostly look – and apply my black eyeliner and mascara. Every week, we'd find something new to wear – either we bought it or knocked it up on the spur of the moment. We went down the King's Road quite a lot, looking in all the shops, and to Harrods. If we couldn't afford it, we made it. I remember sewing together a hobble skirt with a split up the back at the last minute, using an old bit of material I'd found. If someone had grabbed hold of it and pulled, it would have fallen to pieces, but thankfully it survived the evening.

My dad never saw it; he never saw anything! He wouldn't have let me go out in a skirt so tight I could barely walk. He was a bit Victorian in that way. As we left the house, I'd shout out, 'See you later!' and we'd be off before anyone could see us.

After a while, me and Jennifer began to knock about in a crowd. It all started when we began going to a little club in Peckham called the Top Twenty. We ended up going there most weeks and soon made friends with a load of boys who also went regularly. At the weekend we'd bump into them again in Peckham High Street or the arcade, get chatting, go to a coffee bar and arrange to meet later.

'You going to the Co-op?'

'Yeah, see you there!'

If I didn't dance with Jennifer, I'd dance with one of the Peckham boys. You could ask a boy to dance if you wanted to; you didn't have to wait to be asked. They were all good dancers: Fred Perkins, Cedric 'Dinger' Bell, Johnny Oxford and Micky Peabody. If we missed the last bus and had to walk home, they would always walk us there, to make sure we were safe. There was nothing in it apart from friendship, though. It was all very innocent and no one went off with anybody. None of us had boyfriends or girlfriends. They just saw us home.

One Sunday, we were late leaving the Lyceum and I started to panic that my dad would catch me coming in after eleven o'clock. So we hitched a lift with Cedric and Charlie on their Vespa GS scooters. On the way back, me and Cedric had a bit of an accident and I fell off and broke the heel of my shoe. I had to tell my mum I'd fallen off the bus, because I couldn't admit I'd been on a scooter. She didn't like the thought of me on a bicycle, let alone a motorbike!

I loved going on the back of those scooters. Me and Jennifer started going down to the Kent coast with the boys at weekends. One Friday in the summer of 1961, we went to Leysdown with a crowd of fellas for a weekend in a caravan. None of them tried it on. They knew that we'd tell them to piss off if they did, because we weren't into all that.

When we got up the next day, my lower back was feeling really tender. I must have slept in a weird position, I thought.

We all went down the beach. 'Let's go roller skating,' someone said.

Oh dear, I thought. My back's killing me. But I went, anyway.

We rented some roller skates and I tried to have a go at skating, doing my best to ignore the pain. Suddenly, the wheels came off one of my skates and I slipped and fell flat on my back. God, I was in so much pain! I thought I'd broken my back.

The boys picked me up and carried me off to the nearest hospital, where they plonked me on a trolley and pushed me through some double doors. What happened next was like a scene out of a *Carry On* film: I whizzed straight through the ward and out the other side into a long corridor. As I passed all the patients in their beds, I heard people saying, 'Hey!' and, 'What the...?'

A nurse came out of a side room and grabbed hold of the trolley. 'What's happening here?' she said.

'My friends just pushed me through those doors!' I explained, in a fit of nervous giggles. 'My back's killing me.'

It turned out that a big abscess had come up on the coccyx at the base of my spine. I was given penicillin to take until it burst. I had to go home on the train. I could hardly walk for days. I couldn't sit down; I couldn't do anything. In the end I had it lanced at the local hospital, which was as painful and nasty as it sounds.

When I recovered, it was back on the scooters for more larks at Leysdown. This time, we all went dressed up in mad clothes, for a laugh. I can remember exactly what I was wearing: leopardskin trousers with bald knees, where the fur had worn off; winklepicker boots; a moulting fur coat tied up with a stocking; and a big hat with corks hanging down off it.

I was on the back of Micky's scooter on the way home. Unfortunately, it broke down half way there. It was a bit of a walk to get help and somewhere along the line he went his way and I went mine. Left on my own, I had to come back by train from Leysdown. Oh God, I was so embarrassed! I took the hat off, but I did everything I could to hide my face because I was convinced everybody was looking at me as though I was a tramp.

I got into some funny old scrapes, especially when I was with Jennifer. In the summer of 1962, we spent a week at Warners Holiday Camp in Dovercourt Bay. I'll never forget the journey down there on the coach. We decided to make out we were French and sat next to each other talking gobbledegook in a French accent, with the occasional real French word thrown in.

'Au Paree, je dro dre dra.'

'Oui! Sont les peux de don!'

We weren't making any sense at all, but it was clear that the people in the seats next to us had fallen for our act. They were nudging each other and I heard one of them say something about us being 'continental'.

'I hope we don't see them again when we get to Warners,' I whispered to Jennifer, after half an hour of Frenchifying. 'We can't keep this up for a week!'

Well, blow me down, if they weren't sitting on our table in the dining hall! Out of all the people in the whole holiday camp, they had to be the ones sitting with us! As a result, we had to time our every meal to make sure we didn't meet over lunch or dinner. That meant waiting around outside the dining hall until they'd left the table, when we'd slip inside, sit down and have our food. Of course, whenever we walked past them, we had to go back into our made-up French dialogue. They didn't know; they didn't have a clue that we weren't speaking real French. But it was a nightmare having to be on alert the whole time and we ended up wishing we'd never started it. Still, we had a good time. We had a laugh wherever we were.

Jennifer started going out with boys quite a while before I did. She was more advanced than I was, but it didn't matter to me that I didn't have a boyfriend. I was happy enough hanging about with my friends and dreaming of Elvis and Johnny Rae. But I was always restless to go out. I couldn't bear staying in on a Friday or Saturday night, so if ever Jennifer wasn't around, I'd wander over to the Sombrero coffee shop, just for something to do.

She was away the weekend I met Gerald. She'd gone off down to Brighton with some bloke, leaving me to kick my heels. Friday evening at home stretched before me in a boring haze of dullness, so I did my hair in a pleat, put on my make-up, changed into my jeans and a blouse and went over to the Sombrero.

One of the boys I went dancing with was there, Charlie. I got chatting to him and his mate and they bought me a coffee. While we were talking, a good-looking bloke in a blue serge suit strutted towards us. I noticed him looking me up and down. 'This is my big brother, Gerald,' Charlie said.

'Hello darling, who are you?' Gerald said cockily, his grey eyes twinkling.

I said, 'My name's Maureen and I live round the corner. Some people call me Mogsy.'

'Do you want a coffee?'

'Yeah, all right then.'

We had a coffee and went on chatting. 'Would you like to come out for a drink?' he asked.

'When?' I asked. I was going to say no if he suggested the following weekend, because Jennifer would be back by then and we'd be going dancing.

'How about tomorrow?' he said.

Sod me, I thought. I've got nowhere else to go. 'All right then,' I said.

At twenty-two, Gerald was quite a bit older than the boys I went around with. They were just teenagers, like me, but Gerald was a grown bloke, one of the chaps, and in those days you were a cool cat if you went out with someone older than you. We went to the Five Bells pub that first time. One thing led to another and the next thing I knew, I was going out with him.

He was my first boyfriend, the first person I kissed. A couple of months later, we had sex, in the passage at home, up against the door. It was a classic knee trembler, but I didn't enjoy it, and it was my bad luck to get pregnant the very first time I had sex. I missed a period, then I missed another and my breasts swelled up. I wasn't stupid. I knew what it meant.

Mum was in the kitchen when I broke the news. 'I think I'm pregnant, Mum,' I said.

'What?' She couldn't believe her ears.

'Yeah, I think I'm pregnant.'

'Oh dear,' she said, sitting down heavily on one of the kitchen chairs. 'What are we going to do? I wonder what your father will say.'

'I don't know what to say to him,' I said, a feeling of dread washing over me. I knew how disappointed he would be.

'And what will the neighbours say?' Mum added.

'Sod the bleedin' neighbours!' I said angrily. They were the least of my worries.

'Have you been to the doctor's?'

'Not yet.'

I went to see the doctor that afternoon. He pressed my stomach with his fingers. 'Yes, you're pregnant,' he said. 'You'd better make an appointment with the hospital.'

I told Dad when he came home from work. He was upset more than angry. 'You're so young!' he said sadly. 'You're only seventeen. You haven't lived yet.' He got used to the idea in time, but I always felt I'd let him down.

Gerald didn't say much when I told him. He told his mum and dad and they were upset about it, just like my mum and dad were. But it was just one of those things. There was nothing you could do in those days. There were probably pills and potions you could take, but going down that route was dangerous and illegal.

We got married at Amersham Vale Register Office in September 1963. It was so strange, so quick. Gerald was the first bloke I'd been with and suddenly we were married. I didn't love him and he didn't love me. We got married because I was pregnant. It was what you had to do then, to save face. Afterwards, I went on living at home and he lived at his parents' house round the corner, until we got our own place, a flat in Rectory Buildings, Deptford. I stopped going out to dance clubs. We never went dancing. If we went out, we'd go with his mum and dad to a pub.

I quickly came round to the idea of having a baby. I went up St Alfege's Hospital in Greenwich, where they did a urine test, weighed me and gave me a packet of black iron tablets. That was the sum of my antenatal care! Pregnant women didn't have regular examinations or scans then. I went away and grew and waited. By nine months, I was massive. I was so big that I could balance a cup and saucer on my belly while I was standing up.

By now, I was really looking forward to seeing and holding my baby. I went back to the clinic at the hospital and they said, 'Right, we'll book you in. When the pains start, call an ambulance. Don't forget your hospital bag. Here's what you need to bring with you.' They gave me a list and that was that.

The pains started one Friday in January 1964. They eased off for a bit and came back hard on the Saturday night. On Sunday they became really bad and I called an ambulance. At the hospital, they put me into a bed and pulled a curtain around it. 'When you feel more pain, shout out and someone will come,' one of the nurses said.

All around me, I could hear women being sick, moaning and screaming. It put me right off having the baby. 'I don't want it now!' I thought.

I longed for my mum to be with me, but you weren't allowed visitors. 'Birth partners' were unheard of. Your husband wasn't even allowed to be there. You were on your own, apart from the twenty other women in labour around you.

As the pain intensified, I began to feel frightened. Oh God! I thought, gripping on to the iron bedstead for dear life. I gritted my teeth, too scared to make a noise, let alone call for help. I was in a right two and eight by the time my waters broke. I felt small and vulnerable and very, very alone.

A nurse popped her head round the curtain. 'Are you all right?' she asked.

'I don't know. Something's happened,' I said timidly. I had no idea what, though.

She had a quick look and said, 'All right, you're ready!'

Soon I was being wheeled into the labour ward, writhing in silent agony. I hated giving birth. It was an unbelievably painful and lonely experience. I was on my own for the rest of the day and all through the night until just before the baby finally arrived the next morning, all seven pounds and twelve ounces of her. Then they stitched me up, wheeled me into a ward in another part of the hospital and put me back into bed.

The birth had been horrible, but I was happy now I had a baby. She was a pretty little thing with a lovely round face. I think she must have had a touch of jaundice, because she looked as though she was suntanned. People started coming in to the room – nurses, midwives, porters, everyone. 'Let's have a look at your baby!' They all oohed and aahed, because she was terribly sweet, a really beautiful little thing.

I was kept in hospital for the next ten days, which was the standard maternity recovery time back then. For three days, I wasn't even allowed to get out of bed! The nurses made me pee in a bedpan, which I hated. It stung like anything because of the stitches. My baby was taken out during the night and only brought back to be fed. I missed her when they took her away, but at the same time it was nice to lie down and not have to worry, knowing that she was being looked after.

My mum and dad were the first people to visit. Mum arrived with the most beautiful baby clothes. She knitted all my baby clothes, in pretty pink, lilac, white and lemon. Everything was delicately made, with fancy cable work.

'What are you going to call her?' Dad asked.

'Tracy,' I said. 'Tracy Joanne.' The name fitted; somehow she looked just like a Tracy.

Next, Gerald came to see us. He seemed pleased with the baby and didn't object to the names I'd chosen for her. We were in an unhappy marriage, but we both loved little Tracy, so it wasn't all bad.

I had no trouble bonding with Tracy. I loved her to bits. I kept her clean and neat and she always wore nice clothes, which wasn't half as easy back then, when you only had terry towelling nappies. It was a lot of work boiling them up in a bucket on the stove and drying them. Then you had to mess around with great big pins and plastic pants with frills. It was terrible. Today, mums have tiny Pampers that just go in the bin once they're dirty. It's so much easier!

There were chutes for the rubbish at Rectory Buildings, where we were living by then. Many a time Tracy had an upset stomach and, if her nappies were really messed up, I'd put them in a bag and throw them down the chute. Sometimes it was just too much to think about boiling them up. I'd rather go out and buy a new lot.

I had a lot of support from my mum. I used to walk from Deptford to her house and back every day. I loved going over there. Mum did all my laundry and I'd eat there most days. Whenever me and Gerald had a row, I'd go back home and stay there a couple of days. Life trundled on. Mum could see I was unhappy, but there was nothing she could do about it and I just got on with it. It was a miserable time. If I could go back, I wouldn't have got married, because, let me tell you, it's a mistake to marry someone you don't love.

chapter five

Hard Knocks

'WHAT'S THE MATTER?' I asked Mum.

It was 1965 and I was twenty years old. Dad was out in Jamaica working on the bauxite plant for a fourth time and Mum and Gary had just got back from visiting him. It was the first time I'd seen them for several months and I could instantly tell something was wrong.

Mum didn't reply. She was bustling round the kitchen, as usual, getting things ready for tea. Suddenly, she let out a long sigh. Something was definitely bothering her. 'What is it?' I asked again.

There was a pause. She lowered her head. 'I've got a feeling your dad's seeing someone,' she said, her voice wavering.

At first I didn't catch her drift. 'What do you mean?' I said.

'Just that. I think he's having an affair,' she said.

I couldn't believe my ears. Dad wouldn't do a thing like that. He loved Mum. 'Why do you think that?' I asked her. It couldn't be true, it just couldn't.

She collapsed into a chair. 'I could tell something was wrong when we arrived in Jamaica,' she said wearily. 'Your dad just weren't the same. He seemed on edge. I couldn't pin him down to any arrangements. He was vague about everything.'

'Maybe he had something on his mind,' I said.

'That's what I thought at first. I left him to get on with it for a few days. But we hardly ever saw him. "What's going on?" I asked him. "You hardly ever come back to the hotel and Gary's missing his dad." He didn't seem bothered, though. He kept making excuses why he had to be here, there and everywhere.'

It didn't sound like Dad. He was usually such a homebody. Mum went on to say that there had been a bit of a scene one night at the club they used to go to. Apparently Dad introduced her to a couple he knew, a bloke who owned a flying school and his wife. Mum could tell instantly that there was something funny going on with the wife. She was very nervy and wouldn't look Mum in the eye. Later, Mum saw her whisper something to my dad. A few minutes after that, she saw her run outside in tears. Mum said it was obvious there was something between them.

'Did you ask Dad about it?' I asked her.

'He told me not to be silly. She's just his friend, apparently. But my gut feeling told me different.'

'Come on, Mum!' I said. 'Could you be imagining it?'

'Nah, I'm pretty sure,' she said, brushing away a tear. 'It wasn't just that night. There was other things that didn't add up. I just hope he comes to his senses and comes home soon.'

'When's he due back?'

'I don't know,' she said. 'That's something else he was vague about.'

I felt sorry for Mum and did my best to comfort her. I wished Dad would come home and make everything all right. Over the next few months, Mum had a few letters from him, but he was never specific about when he was coming back. All we could do was hope it would be soon. Mum tried to hide her worry, but it was obvious to me that she was anxious. And Gary kept asking, 'When's my dad coming home?'

One evening, Mum phoned me, sounding terrible. 'It's your dad,' she said.

My heart skipped a beat. 'What about him? What's happened?' I asked, fearing the worst.

She dropped a bombshell. 'Turns out he's been back in England for months, living somewhere near Canterbury with that woman.'

I gasped. It had to be a lie. 'Who told you that?' I asked.

'I had this peculiar feeling that something was up with him,' she said. 'So I went up to his work today to ask them if they'd heard from him. I spoke to one of the managers. His face dropped when I asked about your dad. He didn't know where to look. He said, "Didn't you know? He's been back from Jamaica for months."'

I could tell Mum was in a right two and eight, but I couldn't fully take in what she was saying. 'What about the letters?' I asked. How could Dad send letters from Jamaica when he wasn't there? It didn't make sense.

'I don't know, love,' Mum said, sounding tired. 'He must have got someone to send them for him.'

My mind was spinning. 'Do you think he'll come home soon?' I asked.

'I doubt it,' Mum said. 'I think that's it, love,' she added sadly. 'He's left us.'

Dad came up from Canterbury to 'collect his things' a week later. He told Mum he was leaving her, said goodbye and that was that. It was terrible for her. She was devastated. We were all devastated. What would Mum do? How would she survive? My dad didn't seem to care, which hurt us all.

I felt very sad for Gary, who was only seven. I was twenty and had my own life, if you could call it that. Jackie had just married her boyfriend and was expecting a baby. Me and my sister didn't need a dad as much as Gary did. He took it very badly, poor kid.

Dad leaving ripped a hole in all of our lives. I don't think anything ever filled the gap, for any of us. We never got over it. I used to torture myself wondering why he didn't get in contact with me or Jackie. Didn't he love us any more? It was one thing to leave Mum, but why didn't he want to see his children? Gary had been the apple of his eye, his treasured boy, until he'd gone to Jamaica a year before. He did every-thing with him, taking him out at weekends and making things with him at home. So how could he just up and leave him? I couldn't understand it then and I still don't under-stand it today. It's almost as if he was bewitched.

As the months passed, we found things out in dribs and drabs. Dad's new partner was called Pat. She was English, but had been living in Jamaica for many years. Dad had met her the first time he ever went there, when she was just a teenager. But he only got close to her the third time he was there, before Mum and Gary went out to visit. Apparently, her husband had kept saying to him, 'I'm tied up working at the flying school this weekend. Why don't you come down and take Pat and the kids out?' That's how one thing led to another. What was the husband thinking? Didn't he realise he was setting them up?

It was a big knock for my mum. I used to have her and Gary over to stay at our house in Bermondsey and I'd hear Mum crying in the night. She was inconsolable. Dad was the love of her life. It tore me apart to hear her crying. I used to get really upset too. I still thought of myself as a Daddy's girl in a way, and my heart ached at the loss of him. Now he was gone, he would never rescue me from my miserable marriage. Not that I ever really expected him to rescue me, but I never thought he'd abandon us all, either. It was a terrible time.

None of us heard from him. He didn't remember our birthdays. He didn't send a card at Christmas. It was like he was dead, even though he was alive. It took us a long time to come to terms with it. We all missed him so much. So many unanswered questions remained. Why? How could he? But we didn't talk about him much. What was there to say? Dad was gone. That was the end of it. We just had to get on with it.

Life went on. We focused our attention on the kids. We did our best to soften the pain of Dad's absence for Gary by taking him out and buying him things. I suppose we spoilt him. He was a funny kid, always singing. Like me, he did impersonations. He was great at different accents and he took off the Beatles really well. Like my mum, he was clever and loved books. He spent hours reading in his room and when he didn't have his head in a book, he was learning to play the piano. Slowly he was turning into this person who wanted to become an actor. Meanwhile, my daughter Tracy was growing from a baby to a toddler. It wasn't long before she was singing and dancing to 'Big Spender' and other Shirley Bassey songs. She was a bit of a character, my Tracy.

Speaking of characters, one day I got chatting to a small, bubbly blonde called Jan in the launderette and before long she became a firm friend. Right from the start, she called me Mo, and the name stuck. Jan lived around the corner from me, in Rotherhithe New Road, with her husband and kids. They had six children between them – two of hers, three of his and the child they had together. Later they moved to a big block of flats with walkways, the Bonomi at the top of Rotherhithe New Road. It was quite nice, really, but it's not there any more. It was knocked down in the nineties, I think. Me and Jan started going out together, but only when Gerald wasn't around. We had a lot of fun together. She was a real laugh to be with and my life felt a lot brighter when she was around.

I was very grateful for my friendship with Jan, because my days often felt quite empty, especially as I didn't work while Tracy was a youngster. I never went short, but I didn't have a lot of money off Gerald. He would never tell me anything, so I didn't know what he did or how he made his money. I knew nothing about what he got up to outside the house, and I didn't ask questions. I relied on him totally for money, so it was difficult for me to help my mum out, although I did my best by having her to stay at weekends. She claimed family allowance at first and then found herself a job at Selfridges, the big London department store. At forty-six years old, after more than twenty years as a housewife, she was starting afresh. It can't have been easy for her, but she plodded on and soon found that she liked what she did.

Almost five years after Tracy was born, I gave birth to a baby boy. Since I couldn't bear the idea of going into hospital after what had happened with Tracy, I had him at home in my bed, with a really lovely midwife to oversee everything while my mum took care of Tracy downstairs. Gerry weighed eight pounds two ounces, but this time it was a fairly easy birth, or at least it wasn't too bad. It was lovely to have a boy. Now I had one of each.

Gerald wanted him to be called Gerald, and so did his family. 'No, not Gerald,' I said. 'If he's called anything, it will have to be Gerry.' And so Gerry it was.

He was a sweet baby and I loved him from the moment I clapped eyes on him. He always had beautiful clothes – lovely yellow, white and blue babygros – and I went to town buying a beautiful pram. Mum helped me out and I bought things off the book, on the never-never, paying a small amount a week.

Tracy was very excited to have a brother. When he was three days old, she came into my room and said, 'Can I go over and see him?'

'Yeah, but don't poke him or anything, will you?'

'No!'

I was sitting in bed, talking to Jan, when all of a sudden I could hear baby Gerry trying to catch his breath.

'What have you done to him?' I asked Tracy sharply.

'Well, he don't like that mustard pickle!' she said. She'd dipped his dummy in mustard pickle and given it to him. He was three days old!

I laugh about it now, but it worried me at the time. 'You shouldn't do things like that, Tracy,' I scolded gently. 'That's naughty.' I picked Gerry up, patted his back and gave him some boiled water. When he went to the toilet an hour later, it was bright green, and he had the gripes for days. Still, she didn't know, did she?

Five days after Gerry was born, Gerald went to prison for several years. I divorced him while he was in there. I'd had enough of being unhappily married – and so must he have done, because he signed the divorce papers without a word of complaint. That was that for me and Gerald, the end of a miserable chapter in my life.

I stayed in the house in Bermondsey for a few months after Gerald went away, although I was always up at Jan's house or staying with my mum in New Cross. With Gerald away, there wasn't any rush to move on. Gerry was just a tiny baby, after all.

My nan was often at my mum's and it was nice for her to spend time with Tracy and Gerry. By now she was getting on in age and had become a little bit eccentric. She was obsessive about cleanliness in later life; there was never a speck of dirt or dust in her house and she polished her sink and gave it a shine every time she used it.

At night, she was visited by Uncle Billy, who used to sit on the end of her bed and talk to her. 'Hurry up!' he'd say. 'It's about time you came and joined me.'

I heard her talking to Billy a couple of times, when I was staying at Mum's. 'All in good time,' she'd say. 'When I'm ready, I'll be there.'

She was well into her eighties, so we weren't surprised when she developed a touch of bronchitis. It wasn't serious, but she started talking about death. 'Billy keeps calling me,' she told my mum. 'I'll be off to see him soon.'

'Don't be silly!' my mum would say. 'You've got years left in you yet.'

The bronchitis was persistent, so Nan's doctor decided she'd be best off getting checked in hospital. 'I saw Billy last night,' she said, the morning she went in. 'He's calling me again. He's getting impatient. I'll have to go and meet him soon.'

'Nonsense,' Mum said. 'You've got a nasty cough, that's all.'

The doctors in hospital certainly didn't think Nan was close to death, but she was taken for an X-ray, just to make sure her chest was clear. 'I can see Billy,' she told Mum, just before she was wheeled off. 'He's beckoning me.'

Nan was fine when she was wheeled into the patient lift in a trolley; she was her usual chirpy self. But for no apparent reason and to everyone's mystification, she had died by the time she reached the X-ray room. She lay down and her heart stopped beating.

Mum was really upset. We all were. She was a lovely nan. She was really funny and made us laugh all the time. I loved going and staying with her when I was a child and it had been touching to see the way she doted on Tracy and Gerry. We had some really good times before she died. I didn't go to her funeral, though. I don't do funerals, never have. I just don't like the idea of them.

My old friend Prim got in touch to say how sorry she was about Nan's passing. I hadn't heard from her in a while. 'Your nan was amazing,' she said. 'My mum never got over the time she predicted her visit to Reg, when he was ill.'

'What happened?' I asked. I couldn't remember this particular time that Nan had used her psychic powers.

According to Prim, Nan had read Ivy's tea leaves and said, 'A bloke in a uniform is going to knock on your door and ask you to go with him to meet a relative over a bridge.'

'I wonder if it could be something to do with Reg,' Ivy mused. Reg, one of Prim's four brothers, had recently joined the army.

A few weeks later, the knock came at the door. When Ivy answered it, a soldier told her that Reg had been taken ill somewhere near Bristol. She quickly threw a few things together and went with the soldier to visit Reg in hospital. The journey took her over the Clifton Suspension Bridge, one of the biggest bridges in England!

'She obviously had a gift,' Prim said.

'Well, she ain't passed it on,' I said glumly. 'I haven't got a clue what the future holds for me.'

And if I thought about it, the future didn't look too bright. I didn't have an income and couldn't work, because Gerry was just a baby, so I survived on the little money Gerald had left for me and hoped for the best. The kids took up a lot of my time, of course, but at least my mum was always happy to babysit them when I needed a night off. I didn't go out much of an evening, just to the occasional bingo night or a singsong at the pub. But I'd get dressed up all the same, in a mini skirt or suede hotpants, with false eyelashes top and bottom. You never went out without your eyelashes on. I didn't get into all the long hippy dresses that came out at the end of the sixties; I stuck to shorter hemlines and high-legged boots.

Whenever I did go out and I called a minicab, I noticed that I kept getting the same driver in the same green Ford Zephyr. Tall and stocky, with brown hair and dark, velvety eyes, he was a good-looking bloke and his name was George. One evening, we got chatting and he asked me out. 'I can't. I'm married,' I told him. I didn't say I was planning to get divorced, because I hadn't started the proceedings yet. I kept quiet about all that. One step at a time.

A few months later, George asked me out again. Since I'd put in for a divorce by then, I said I'd think about it. Finally, I agreed to go out with him. He picked me up in his other car, a white TR4 convertible, and we had a good night. After that, I started seeing him on a regular basis.

Truth is, George swept me off my feet. He told me I was the most beautiful girl he'd ever met and I fell in love with him straight away. For months and months, I'd get a chirpy stomach every time the phone rang, or he picked me up in the car. As well as being good looking, he was gentle and nice and took me out all over London, to the East End and the West End, to different pubs and restaurants. Being with him gave me a nice, warm feeling. It was the first time I'd ever felt that way with someone.

George made me feel special – and it was fantastic to feel special. The combination of an unhappy relationship and my dad leaving us had left me with very low self-esteem. I had gone from being a cheeky, outgoing youngster to being quite introverted and shy. I had very little self-worth, so I felt lucky to have George in my life. He was only twenty, four years younger than me, but he seemed older and he always had money. He worked hard and I think his mum and dad were quite well off. By night he drove a minicab, by day he had a car front in Bermondsey, where he and his partner Jas sold used cars. He was generous with his money and bought me all kinds of bits and bobs, from perfume to handbags and shoes. He was really lovely to me.

In time, I moved out of the house in Bermondsey, because I wanted to leave the past behind. For a while, I moved here, there and everywhere, bouncing back and forth between friends. Sometimes the kids were with me, sometimes with my mum. I must have gypsy blood, because I've always liked to move around. I'd do it now if I could.

Eventually, I landed back living with my mum. There was never any question of me living with George, even though we were madly in love. I accepted that it was probably too much for him to take on me and two children. Anyway, he lived with his mum and dad in Bermondsey. He came to stay with me at weekends and one or two nights in the week.

I didn't meet his parents for a long time after I started seeing him. I don't know why. He just didn't introduce us. Perhaps his mother was protective of him. His dad was tall and a proper cockney. His mum was Italian and she could hardly speak English, although she'd been in England since the Second World War. I had to speak very clearly when she answered the phone.

"Ello!' she'd say.

'Is George there, please?'

'Uno momento, Big Giorgio or Little Giorgio?'

'It's me, Maureen.'

'Oh, momento!' She'd call to George in a burst of Italian with 'Maureen' somewhere in the middle of it.

It was years before I went up to his house off Jamaica Road in Bermondsey, but eventually I had tea there a couple of times and his mum cooked lovely food. That's probably why he never ate with me at home. He'd come round, stay the night and leave first thing in the morning. I never did his breakfast or cooked him a meal, in all the years I was with him. He ate at his mum's, unless we went out for a meal of an evening. When I look back, it's strange to think that I was with him for so long and never cooked for him.

My mum liked George – at least, I never heard her criticise him or say anything against him – and George was very close to his parents. He understood the importance of family, so when I confided in him and told him about how Dad had left us, he was very sympathetic. 'I still love my dad,' I explained. 'It doesn't matter what he's done; he's still my dad and I miss him every day.'

'Why don't we go down and see if we can find him?' George said. 'I'll take you one evening after work.'

'All right,' I said, my heart leaping. I was desperate to see Dad. I was sure he would relent if I could just talk to him for a few minutes.

George drove me down to Canterbury in the Zephyr. We asked people for directions to the nearest caravan park, where Mum had said Dad was living with Pat. When we finally found it at around nine o'clock, we asked some people at the gate which caravan they were in. It wasn't easy to find it in the dark, but eventually we knocked on the door. My heart was pounding.

Dad answered the door. He looked just the same. 'Hello Dad,' I said.

His face fell. I instantly knew that it wasn't going to be the wonderful reunion I had dreamed of, far from it. He didn't ask us in.

'I've missed you so much,' I said, trying to hold back the tears.

He looked down. 'I'm sorry, Maureen, you'd better go away,' he said. 'I've got a new life now. I don't want to know the family any more.'

I felt like I'd been hit. I tried to catch my breath, but it was like I'd been winded. I took a step backwards, my mind swirling. 'Dad?' I pleaded. He shut the door in my face.

My knees went. I thought I was going to collapse there and then. George put his arm around me. 'Come on, love.

We'd better go,' he said. I don't remember walking back to the car.

I cried all the way home. I was brokenhearted. George did his best to comfort me, but there was nothing he could say to make me feel better. I just couldn't understand why Dad didn't want to know us any more. Why had he been so cold to me? It didn't make any sense.

I didn't know it at the time, but his partner Pat was starting to become ill with multiple sclerosis, a muscle-wasting disease. A long time afterwards, when Dad and Mum got in touch again, I found out that Pat was bedridden within a few years of them getting together. She couldn't speak; she had to spell out words on a blackboard. I think that must have been why Dad wanted to cut off from us, although who can say whether it was out of loyalty, pity or a need for privacy? He never explained his reasons.

It took me a long time to get over what happened that night. I cried myself to sleep for months afterwards. I couldn't understand why Dad had rejected me. We had been so close when I was growing up; I had worshipped and adored him, and I'd always felt loved and treasured by him in return. So why had he turned his back on me now? What had I done wrong? It was devastating to think he no longer cared about me. I felt completely lost.

It was like he had abandoned me all over again.

chapter six

Playing Around

AT LEAST I was happy with George. I had a wonderful time with him for the first seven years we were together. I really loved him. We had a lot of laughs and there was a strong attraction between us.

In the beginning, we were always together. We went out to dinner in candlelit restaurants and to the pictures. We'd meet up with friends in the pub. When he was working, I'd go with him in the car: here, there and everywhere. I'd do anything to spend time with him. I couldn't wait to see him. Often we went out every night of the week and at weekends we'd go off somewhere to stay in a hotel, leaving the kids with my mum. We had some happy times in the New Forest and down in Mevagissey in Cornwall.

When George wasn't around, me and Jan would go out dancing. We had so much fun together. We both had partners, but that didn't stop us being a bit flirty. After all, we were only in our twenties. One Friday night, we were at the Cromwellian Club in Knightsbridge. One of George's haunts, it was an upscale club with a gambling room upstairs and dancing in the basement. I was wearing a velvet mini skirt this particular evening and at one point I was standing up against the wall at the bottom of some stairs, talking to a bloke who had his hands on my hips.

Suddenly, Jan gave me a nudge. 'Don't look now, but George has just walked in with his mates!' she said.

I turned round and saw him. He gave me a terrible look. 'You'll have to go,' I said to the bloke. 'My boyfriend's just arrived.'

'All right,' he said, and off he went.

George grabbed hold of me. 'Here, what do you think you're playing at?'

'What you talking about?' I said, my eyes wide with innocence.

'That bloke had his hands on your hips!'

I had to think fast. 'Yeah, he works as a velvet tester and he wanted to check the quality of my skirt!' I said.

He didn't believe me, but I stuck to my story. He didn't have to worry. I might have been flirting a bit, but I was totally faithful to George and he knew it.

Me and Jan always attracted blokes, especially in pubs. We couldn't help it – we were young and blonde and pretty. Sometimes we'd tell them where to go and sometimes we'd let them buy us drinks, depending on our mood. If we did accept their drinks, we'd keep an eye on the clock and just before the lights went on at the end of pub hours, we'd say, 'We won't be long. We're going to the toilet.' Then we'd leave the pub on our hands and knees and rush off home, before they saw us.

We had such a laugh, even when things went wrong. One night, Jan was wearing a little black mini dress that was held together with big plastic hoops. It looked really good with her blonde hair, but when we walked into the club we were going to, it turned out that all the waitresses were wearing the same dress as part of their uniform!

Two minutes after we arrived, someone came up and said, 'Could we order some drinks, please?'

'I beg your pardon?' she replied. We had to leave and go somewhere else.

Because we were always together, at one point people thought we were lesbians. I'll never forget the night we were at a pub in Bermondsey and these blokes kept looking at us and whispering. We just knew what they were saying: 'You see them two over there...'

'If they keep looking at us like that, I'm gonna kiss you!' Jan said.

A few seconds later, she grabbed my face and kissed me hard on the cheek near my mouth. Well, one of the blokes watching us happened to be lifting his pint to his lips right at that moment. The sight of our 'lesbian' kiss obviously knocked him off balance, because he poured his drink right down the front of his white shirt. Me and Jan nearly wet ourselves laughing.

At this point, I was still on the move between my mum's house and other addresses around London, including Jan's. Then I got a job – as a cashier in a betting shop in Battersea – and me and the kids spent a couple of years living above the shop. It was the first work I'd done since having children and it felt good to be earning my own money, even though George had always looked after us financially until then. George would come and stay every other night and at weekends, so it didn't matter that I was living quite a way from him.

Gerry was about four when we moved and he was already giving me trouble. He was a naughty child, always doing something he shouldn't, getting into one scrape or another. He was continually wandering off when you weren't looking and then there would be a frantic search to find him.

When Tracy was nine, she took four-year-old Gerry to Victoria with her for a day out. As usual, he wandered off, but this time she lost him. When she came back to Battersea without him, I called the police. They said, 'A person has to be missing for twenty-four hours before we start a search.'

'But he's only four!' I protested. I was out of my mind with worry.

Any other kid would have burst into tears, gone up to an adult and sobbed, 'I've lost my mum!' Not my Gerry. He hopped on a bus, got off at the right stop and found his way back, on his own.

I was so relieved to see him, but angry, too. 'You shouldn't disappear off like that!' I yelled at him.

My mother couldn't help putting in her twopenny's worth. 'You was exactly the same!' she said.

'Yeah, thanks for reminding me, Mum.'

Gerry was a funny, cheeky kid, a real character, but there was also a vulnerable side to him that pulled on my heart-strings. I desperately wanted to protect him from trouble and harm, but he would never listen. I couldn't do enough for him ... but it didn't matter what I did. He just used to run off and do his own thing anyway. He pressed a fair few emergency stop buttons as a child. He couldn't help himself. 'I just wanted to see what would happen,' he'd say.

He didn't like school. Even when he was five, I'd drop him off in the morning and then get a phone call from one of the teachers saying, 'Your son's run off!' I'd have to leave work and run around and find him. He became a constant worry. During the day, he would test my patience to the limit and I'd get really cross with him because he played up so much, but then I used to look in on him when he was asleep at night and think how sweet and lovable he was at heart.

When he was about seven, we went to Brighton with Mum. On the train there, he wandered off and came back with a sandwich for me and Mum. The next thing I knew, a member of British Rail staff had come into the carriage asking us to pay up! That's the type of thing he used to get up to.

In Brighton, he didn't want to eat where me and Mum were going at dinnertime, so Mum gave him some money to go somewhere else. 'Have a good dinner, did you?' we asked when he came back. Little did we know that he had eaten the dinner without paying for it and kept the money!

On the way back, the train was about to pull out of Brighton Station when I noticed Gerry wasn't with us. I got up and went towards the next carriage, only to find that the train didn't have any more carriages in that direction. That's funny, I thought. I could have sworn I saw Gerry going this way.

It turned out that Gerry had gone into the next carriage and pulled the cart pin out from between the carriages, disengaging them. As we pulled away, I saw his little face peering out of a stationary carriage. 'Oh God, my boy's been left behind!' I shouted.

I ran to the window and shouted to Gerry, 'Get on the next train and I'll meet you at Clapham!'

He found his own way, no trouble. You couldn't have lost him if you'd wanted to.

He didn't learn how to read and write at school, because he was never there. 'You must learn to read!' I told him, over and over again. 'Otherwise, you'll never be able to go anywhere, because you have to be able to read signs to know where you're going.' It didn't make any difference. He still hopped the wagon at every opportunity.

It was a struggle to cope with two kids on my own and hold down a full-time job. I often felt like I was running around in circles, chasing my own tail. I tried to do my best for them. When I look back, though, I think I could have done things differently. Who doesn't? Fact is, there's no point trying to shut the stable door after the horses have bolted … but if I could do it all again, I would stay at home with my kids a lot more, instead of going out with George so much. At the time, I thought Tracy and Gerry would be fine spending their evenings with their nan, while I spent my free time with George, but they probably needed me to be around more.

I try not to blame myself. I was very young and I didn't know what I know today. Isn't that the way of life? By the time you're old enough to have got a bit of wisdom between your ears, it's far too late to put it into practice. To tell the truth, I was so madly in love that I put my relationship first too often. I can say that now. It's too late for regrets, but in my heart of hearts, and with the benefit of hindsight, I can't help feeling that I didn't do enough for my children.

I had a lot of arguments with George about Gerry. Tracy got on with George up to a point; there was definitely affection there. He used to sit on the floor and massage her feet while she massaged the bald patch on his head. Seeing them always reminded me of how I used to comb my dad's hair. But Gerry and George didn't like each other. George was very tough on my boy. He was always telling him off. 'Stop slamming the car door!' he'd yell. 'You can't eat crisps in the car!' It was 'Don't do this!' and 'Don't do that!' He was constantly on his case. I didn't like that at all. It tore me apart and we often rowed over it. There would be murders when he was nasty to him in front of me. Even when Gerry was little, George used to take his dummies out of his mouth and stamp on them. He never liked him. I suppose it was because he was a boy. He was nicer to him as he grew older, though.

We left Battersea when I was given a council place back in Bermondsey, in a block called Bowman House. I made it really nice; I bought beautiful blinds and curtains; I furnished the rooms with comfortable furniture; I painted the walls and built a wooden fireplace; and I often browsed in little antique shops, picking up bits and bobs. It looked great by the time I'd finished with it, although it was too small to be my perfect home. Ideally, I'd have lived in a massive loft apartment with simple, minimal furniture, open brickwork, a spiral staircase and beautiful art on the wall. But that's another story.

By now, I was driving a van for Guy's Hospital, delivering blood samples, vaccines and medicines to different clinics around London. It was much better than being stuck in an office job. I preferred to be on the move and it meant I could pop in and see George when I passed his car front during the day. The job was fairly well paid, but the money never seemed to stretch as far as I needed it to. Fortunately, George was quite generous with me and often helped me out.

One evening he turned up at the flat with a beaming smile on his face. He looked incredibly pleased with himself. 'What's going on?' I asked.

'Fancy going on holiday?' he said.

'Why? Where?'

He grinned. 'I've just bought a place in Lanzarote.'

'Have ya?'

'So, let's all go next week. You, me, Tracy and Gerry.'

It was a lovely apartment in Puerto del Carmen and we had some really nice times out there. For the next few years, we went there quite a bit, about three times a year. They were good holidays, despite George and Gerry not getting on. George was never tight with his money; we didn't want for anything when we were away. We went sightseeing and explored the island, up to the caves in the mountains and to hidden coves along the coast. George loved fishing on the rocks.

Tracy and Gerry made friends in the local town. One day, in typical teenage fashion, Tracy was in the town hanging about with some English and Spanish teenagers when someone offered her a puff on a wacky-baccy. It didn't agree with her at all. After a few drags, she began to feel awful. She didn't know what day it was and she was dying for a drink of water. Somehow she staggered home, but it put her off for good. That was the first and last time Tracy tried any kind of drug. She doesn't even smoke cigarettes.

As I've said, George and I were very happy for the first seven years we were together. I thought I'd be with him forever. Then everything changed between us. Suddenly he wasn't the same towards me. I didn't see him as much. He wasn't as nice to me. We didn't do so much together. I noticed that he'd started changing his clothes before he came up to the flat after work. He was always smart, so there was no need for it. Now he'd be smelling nice, wearing something new, then saying he had to go off and do things.

One Friday night, he came round smelling of aftershave and cologne. 'Where are you going?' I asked suspiciously.

'To play cards.' He wouldn't meet my eye.

'Can't I come?' In previous years, he'd always taken me with him.

'No, it's just the boys tonight. Anyway, I've got to go and look at a house before that.'

My heart sank. I knew it wasn't true. I had a gut feeling.

After it had happened a few times, I realised he was playing around. He'd pop in and I'd say, 'What are you doing later?'

'Having a drink with the boys.'

'You coming back later?'

'No, I doubt it, because I've got to go to work early tomorrow.'

I know what's happening, I thought. It was heartbreaking.

Once I know what's what, I'll go out of my way to prove it. I knew which pubs he drank in. He always went to the same places. One night he was in one of his regular haunts, the Red Cow. I knew he was in there because I drove past and saw his car. I drove on and parked up the road, so that I could watch both exits and see which door he came out of. I waited there for hours until I finally saw him.

People started leaving the pub at eleven thirty and just before midnight I saw George coming out with a blonde girl. He opened the boot of his car and loaded some wine and beer into it. I waited until he pulled away and I followed him, but he was fast and I lost him. My car was just an old banger, a Ford Consul, no match for his sports car. So I turned and headed for home.

The next thing I knew, I saw him up ahead at the lights. I pulled up right next to him, wound down my window and said, 'Where are you going?'

He tried to hide his dismay. 'To Den's house with the boys.'

'Who's that old tart?' I said, nodding at the girl sitting next to him. I didn't look at her. I was too busy focusing on his face, watching his attempts to look innocent.

'I'm dropping her off on the way,' he said casually.

'That's a lie,' I said.

'What do you mean?' he blustered. 'You're mad! I'm only dropping her off.' He revved the car impatiently.

'You've got to be an idiot to think I'd believe that,' I said. The lights changed to green and he shot away. I knew there was no way I'd catch him, so I went home.

Another time, I plotted up outside a club called J Arthurs and waited and waited until he finally came out. Again, he was with a bird. I tried to follow him, but he soon lost me. It didn't matter, though. Now I knew for sure. George was a playboy.

It went on for years and years, but he always denied it. He said I was imagining it. I knew I wasn't. I became very obser-vant. I was a bit of a spy. I'd get in the car and see long blonde hairs on the passenger seat. I couldn't leave him, though. I kept hanging on to the memory of the good times we'd had, hoping that we could be happy again. And he always managed to charm me back. He had a magnetism about him that made everything all right while I was with him.

He'd go away with his mates on holiday and I tortured myself with thoughts of what he'd be getting up to. I couldn't trust him for a minute. When I didn't see him, my mind would be racing, wondering who he was with, going over our conversations and trying to work out the truth from the lies. Then he would appear at the door and everything would be all right again.

He was very persuasive. 'Don't be mad, Mo,' he'd say. 'You're the only one for me, always have been since the day I clapped eyes on you. Do you really think I could look at another woman when I've got you, the most beautiful girl in the world? No, never. You're more than enough woman for me. You're smashing.'

But it wasn't the same any more. I didn't feel the way I had in the early years. He didn't either, or he wouldn't have been going off with other people. Yet at the same time, he didn't want me to be with anybody else. He was extremely jealous and possessive, even though he was the unfaithful one. He came to stay now and again, but it wasn't on a regular basis any more. It was just when it suited him. I wanted to break up with him, but he wouldn't let me. We'd have a row and I'd say I wanted it to end, but he didn't take a blind bit of notice.

Thankfully, I had Jan to go out and have fun with. It was good to be able to let my hair down and do a bit of flirting, with my bubbly mate by my side. I was very upfront with blokes, though. I didn't lead them on. If a bloke started saying, 'Do you want to go out for a drink, or a meal?' I'd say, 'If you think you're taking me home to get my knickers off, you're on the wrong track, mate!'

I knew what they were after and I didn't want to put up with all the palaver of going out to dinner, only to turn them down at the end of the evening. So I let them know beforehand. I never heard from them again, so there you are! They only wanted to take me out to get in my knickers.

I made another good friend in Sue, who lived next door to us at Bowman House. My brother Gary gave Sue the nickname 'Karate Sue', after we went to karate lessons at the library in Brunel Road. We only went for a few weeks, but the nickname stuck for decades! We didn't go out much though, because her partner Dave was a bit of a nuisance. He was quite demanding and she spoiled him by doing everything for him. He had a little bell that he rang when he wanted her to do something for him. 'Sue-Sooze!' he'd call out. 'Answer the phone!' or 'Where's my dinner?' She'd come into my flat for a chat and within ten minutes he'd knock on the window. 'Come on, I want me tea!' he'd say.

She couldn't go anywhere without him saying, 'Where you been? You took too long!' Still, we managed to have a laugh together when he wasn't around. I was always complaining to her about how naughty Gerry was and she usually helped me to see the funny side, if there was one. She was very fond of my kids and still is, to this day.

Meanwhile, George bought a rundown house in Sidcup and started doing it up. When he took me to see it, I noticed there was a brand-new big bed in the main bedroom. That rang alarm bells. Why do you want a bed in a place that isn't done up?

One night, I couldn't sleep. I kept going over what George had told me earlier in the evening. Something didn't add up. 'Are you staying here tonight?' I'd asked him.

'I can't,' he said. 'I've got to meet a bloke in Sidcup about doing work on the house,' he said.

'So you're staying there?'

'Nah, I'll go home to my mum's,' he said.

A little later, he mentioned that he needed to go to a builder's yard in Sidcup in the morning. 'So you're going to Sidcup tonight, to your mum's to sleep and back to Sidcup in the morning? Even though you're getting up early to go to work?' I couldn't help trying to catch him out.

He looked confused for a moment, so I knew I was on to something. 'Yeah, what of it?' he said. 'Have you suddenly turned into my parole officer?'

'Why would you need a parole officer?' I asked. 'What you done wrong?'

'Nothing,' he said, looking irritated. 'You know I ain't.'

As I lay in bed that night, unable to sleep, I had a strong gut feeling that George was up to his tricks again. But I needed to know for sure. I got up and threw some clothes on. Then I went into Gerry's room – Tracy was at my mum's – woke him up and said, 'Come on, we're going to Sidcup.'

As I drove past the house, I saw George's car in the driveway. He had a beige Mercedes then; the TR4 was long gone. I told Gerry to wait in the car. He was still only half awake, so he was happy to lie down on the back seat and go to sleep. I tried George's car door. It was locked. So I marched up to the house and banged on the front door. 'George!' I shouted. 'I know you're in there. You fucking bastard, get down here!'

I could hear scuffling behind the door, the sound of feet on the floorboards of an empty house. A few minutes later, George opened the door. I looked over his shoulder into the dark house. There was a bird in the kitchen behind him. 'What's going on?' he yelled.

'"What's going on?"' I repeated incredulously. It was obvious, wasn't it?

The bird piped up in turn. 'What's going on, George?' she asked.

It was too much for me. Something snapped and I ran into the house and upstairs into the bedroom. I felt the bed. It was still warm. I raced downstairs into the kitchen and went for her. 'See ya!' I told her, and I punched her in the face.

'Let's go!' George shouted. She made a run for the door and I chased after her. Outside the house, as she hurriedly got into George's car, I kicked her and called her every kind of dirty slag insult you can think of; every nasty name under the sun. George started the car and they sped off down the road.

Just then, the next-door neighbour came out to see what was going on. It was lucky that he did, because my car wouldn't start. 'What's all the shouting about?' he asked.

'Can I borrow your jump leads?' I said, and sorted it out.

Amazingly, Gerry slept through the whole thing. He woke up on the journey home. 'What happened, Mum?' he asked.

'Nothing,' I said shortly. 'Go back to sleep.'

When I finally made it home and got into bed, I couldn't nod off. I was fuming. Finally, I had caught George red-handed but he still refused to admit what he was up to.

I decided to confront him once and for all, so I went to his car front the following day. 'What's your game?' I asked angrily.

He scrunched his face up, as if he hadn't a clue what I was talking about. 'What?'

'Having that old tart there. I know you copped hold of her. You had her there and you slept with her.'

He looked at me like I was barmy. 'That's ridiculous. You've lost your mind!' he said.

'What was she doing there, then?'

'Look, she was out with her mates and they left her and she couldn't get home. I took her back to the house for a cup of tea. Then I was going to give her a lift home.'

He expected me to believe him.

That's when I started to turn. Suddenly I'd had enough of all his lies. 'You know what?' I said. 'Let's call it a day.'

'What are you talking about?' he said. 'Don't be stupid. You've let your imagination run away with you, you silly cow. But you shouldn't have. You know you're the only one for me.'

I shook my head. 'It won't work this time, George,' I said. 'I've had enough.'

He wouldn't listen. He simply refused to break up with me. Later that day, he came round to the flat as if nothing had happened. A couple of days after that, he turned up with a bottle of my favourite perfume. I tried to send him away, but he wouldn't take no for an answer.

Against my better judgment, we slipped back into our routine. He acted as if nothing had changed, but I was miserable.

chapter seven

Led Astray

I COULD SMELL it the moment I walked into the flat. The whole place stank of it. My heart sank. Not again, I thought. 'Gerry!' I yelled. 'Come here! I know what you've been doing.'

There was no answer. I ran around the flat, frantically looking for him. He wasn't in his bedroom, or the bathroom. 'Tracy, where's Gerry?' I called. Again, no answer. She was supposed to be looking after him, but she wasn't at home, either.

Looking for further proof, I rifled through Gerry's bedroom. Nothing. I opened the drawer of a chest on the landing. Nothing. I opened another drawer. Bingo. There were two sticky crisp bags hidden under a pile of clothes. 'I knew it!' I muttered. 'He's been sniffing glue out of empty crisp packets again.'

Without bothering to take off my coat, I ran out of the front door and into the street. 'Gerry!' I shouted. 'Where are you?' My heart was pounding. He was only nine years old. What if something had happened to him?

Despite his young age, my son was already in big trouble. He was mixing with a lot of kids in the area who were older than him. They'd got him into the glue – and that wasn't the half of it. He was only little, just the right size for squeezing through tight gaps and spaces, so they were using him to break into buildings and steal things. I'd had visits from the police and I was constantly getting phone calls from his school to say that he'd hopped it, or hadn't turned up that day. I'd warned him, I'd threatened him, but nothing I said made any difference. 'If this doesn't stop, you'll go to prison,' I'd say. 'If you go on sniffing glue, you'll wind up dead.' But he didn't listen. He was running wild and I just couldn't seem to do anything stop him.

I don't know how I coped with it all. I just did. It was something I had to try and tackle, on my own. I used to clump him and Tracy across the legs with a plastic spatula if they misbehaved – and it used to sting like anything. Yet it didn't do any good. I tried to keep them in, but I couldn't. Tracy didn't cause me any serious trouble, but Gerry was another matter.

I passed a group of older boys on the street corner. 'Have you seen my Gerry?' I asked them.

'Nah,' one of them said. He took a drag on his cigarette, blew the smoke right in my face and turned away.

Just along the road, I saw two boyish figures in a doorway, huddled up and laughing weakly. 'Gerry, you little sod,' I yelled, pouncing on him. I grabbed him by his coat and pulled him out of the doorway. In the glare of the streetlight, I could see that his eyes were glazed and bloodshot.

'Get off, Mum!' he whined, trying to shake himself free.

'You're coming home with me!' I told him, dragging him along the street. The group of boys on the corner jeered us as we passed them.

Once I'd got him in the house and locked the front door, I threw him down on the sofa. 'You've been at that glue again!' I said.

'I haven't, Mum. Honest!'

I let out a deep sigh. On the outside I was seething, but

inside my heart was breaking. I loved my boy so much. Why was this happening? What had gone wrong?

There was a knock at the door. I went to see who it was. A spotty teenager was standing outside. 'Is Gerry in?' he asked with a smirk.

The sight of him made my blood boil. 'Piss off!' I shouted. 'Go and pick on someone your own age. You've no business coming to call on a little kid. Go on, fuck off out of it. If I see Gerry with you, I'll go round your mother's, or I'll take you all up the police station.' I slammed the door.

Two days later, the police were round again. There had been a break-in at a bonded warehouse in Rotherhithe and they had reason to believe that my Gerry had played a part in it.

It was every mother's nightmare. I'm being punished, I thought.

I was consumed by guilt. I hadn't done anything wrong, but I kept thinking it had to be my fault that Gerry had gone off the rails. Looking back, I think one of the problems was that he didn't have any male role models to follow. Gerry didn't like George. His father wasn't around – and Gerry disliked him, anyway. Gerry and my brother Gary got on well, but Gary was away studying for a degree in drama at Rose Bruford Drama College in Kent, transforming himself into an actor. He wasn't around enough to have an influence. Dad might have helped Gerry if he had still been with Mum, but he was long gone. Mum did get married again briefly, to an Irishman called Patrick, but he died a few years later. So there was no one, really.

By now, I was near breaking point. I was on my own, a single mum, and it was a struggle to earn a living and provide for my kids, let alone cope with glue sniffing and stealing and visits from the police. I was going out of my mind with worry. I kept imagining terrible things happening to Gerry. I couldn't relax. I couldn't focus on my driving job. My anxiety levels were through the roof.

In desperation, I turned to Social Services for help. A social worker suggested trying to find Gerry a place at a state-subsidized boarding school called Barwick House, which was based in Yeovil, Somerset. It had a reputation for strict discipline, he told me. Gerry would be safe there – and out of the reach of the older boys in our area, who were leading him astray. I wasn't very happy about him going so far away, but it seemed like the best option for Gerry. Better a boarding school than a borstal, I decided.

I took him there on the train. He cried all the way. 'Mum, why are you doing this?' he kept saying.

'It's for your own good,' I replied. I said it over and over again, trying to convince myself as much as him. I nearly turned around and headed back to London several times, but that wouldn't have helped him and he desperately needed help. He was totally out of control and there was nothing I could do about it. I'd tried everything to keep him out of trouble, but nothing had worked. I was terrified he'd end up dead. And, if I was completely honest, I needed a break, too. I simply couldn't cope any longer. I was at my wit's end.

I hated the thought of him being shut away, though. I tried to comfort myself with the thought that he was going to a place where he could get off the drugs and learn self-discipline. Yet at the same time, he was still my baby. I was going to miss him terribly, even if he had been running me ragged. But there was no alternative, I told myself. He was his own worst enemy and I couldn't stop his descent into self-destruction, however hard I tried.

Barwick House School certainly looked the business. It was a massive old mansion set in lovely grounds, with a lake and a long driveway leading up to it. As we went through the enormous front door, I was struck by its big hallways, high ceilings and beautiful panelled doors and walls. We were taken into an office for a chat with the headmaster, an ex-army major, before they took my boy away. After an hour, I had to leave.

It was terrible. Gerry was screaming. I was crying. Saying goodbye to him was one of the worst things I've ever had to do. I sobbed my heart out on the journey home.

But at least I didn't have to worry any more. He was safe now, out of harm's way. I couldn't protect him from himself – but maybe boarding school could.

It was painful going to visit Gerry. Barwick House School was a really strict, regimental place where they instilled military-style discipline. He always burst into tears when he saw me and I had to struggle not to cry as well. 'Take me away from here, please, Mum!' he would beg.

'I can't!'

Back at home, the flat felt empty without him. Tracy was nearly sixteen and spending more and more time over in Battersea with her boyfriend and his family, so I found myself living practically alone for the first time in my life. It felt strange. Of course, Gerry came home for the holidays, and sometimes Tracy popped back for a couple of nights or George came over, but I was seeing a lot less of George now than I had been, so I was often on my own in the evenings.

Nearly two years after Gerry went away to school, in 1981, when I was thirty-five, I got a job in the Crystal Tavern, the pub opposite my flat in Bermondsey. I was driving during the day and working in the pub a couple of evenings a week and at lunchtime on the weekends. I loved it because it was so near my flat and I knew a lot of people who went there. It was a sociable job and I got on well with the guv'nor and his two sons. They used to have a lot of 'afters' or 'lock-ins', when the pub would shut and the curtains would be drawn, but the bar would stay open all night for regular punters.

I'd been working there a couple of months when a tall, blond, good-looking guy walked through the door and up to the bar. My heart flipped over at the sight of him and I quickly lowered my eyes. I couldn't bring myself to look at him, let alone take his order.

I turned straight to Linda, who was working behind the bar with me, and said, 'I can't serve him.' I gave a subtle nod in his direction.

'Why ever not?' she asked.

'Because I just can't,' I said firmly.

I turned my back on him and tried to look busy. What's got into me? I thought. I had never seen this guy before – I didn't know him from Adam – but the sight of him had left me reeling. I was bowled over by him, and we hadn't said a word to each other yet!

Later, Linda told me that his name was Jimmy. He was twenty-one and worked with his dad as a waterman (transporting people) and lighterman (transporting goods) on the River Thames, driving freight boats, pleasure boats and hovercrafts. I don't know how I'd missed him, because he was a regular customer at the Crystal Tavern and lived in the flats opposite me. Suddenly he seemed to be in the pub every time I worked there.

For the first week, I made sure somebody else served him when he came in, because my mouth would go dry just looking at him. I couldn't speak to him; I couldn't meet his eye. It was that bad – although I don't think he noticed.

Eventually, I got up the guts to serve him. I blushed and stammered a bit at first, but he was really nice and friendly. In fact, I was surprised at how easy it was to talk to him. After that, we always chatted and had a bit of a flirt when he came in.

One night, I stayed in the bar for afters. Jimmy was there, too – that's probably why I stayed. It was a few weeks after we'd met and we ended up dancing to the George Benson song, 'Give Me The Night'. It didn't go any further than that, though. He never took me home or anything. I had no dealings with him in that way.

By now, George and I were just plodding along. The holidays had dried up and I rarely went away with him. Instead, I started going on holiday with my bubbly blonde mate Jan, just her and me. Her husband was happy to stay at home and look after the kids, whereas George was very possessive and didn't like me going away with Jan. But what could he expect if he didn't go anywhere with me himself?

We had quite a few rows about it. 'I know what you and that tart get up to!' he'd say.

He was wrong about that, though, because we didn't get up to anything much, apart from a bit of topless sunbathing. Like most people on holiday, we were there for the sun and the sea and to get away from it all. Our days were spent looking for somewhere to strip off and sunbathe in peace, away from the crowds and prying eyes.

One time, we were walking along the beach in Ibiza, stopping off every now and again to have a beer. Eventually, we came to a stretch of rock jutting out over the sea. 'This looks nice,' Jan said.

'Yeah, let's sunbathe here,' I said.

Jan took all her clothes off. She wanted an all-over tan. I took my top off, went in swimming, came out and lay on my towel. We must have dropped off to sleep and when I woke up, I could hear a load of Spanish voices. When I looked round, there were about thirty boys and kids fishing off the point of the rock! They must have been off having their siesta when we arrived there and then they'd come back while we were sleeping!

'Don't look now!' I whispered to Jan. 'Just grab your clothes and run!' We legged it off the rock as fast as we could.

That was as racy as it got when me and Jan went away together. Anyway, I had never been with anyone else since I'd met George. More fool me, I often thought, because he was with a different bird every week, or so it sometimes seemed.

In the summer of 1981, Jan and I planned a holiday to Ibiza for a fortnight. We were going to be staying in a villa that we'd booked through a travel agent we found in the paper. As the days flew past and our departure date approached, I started to get really excited. I couldn't wait to get away.

I worked a few extra shifts in the pub that month. About a week before we left, Jimmy came in. 'I'm going on holiday next Saturday,' I blurted out.

His blue eyes lit up. 'Are you? Where?'

'Ibiza, with my friend Jan,' I said. 'Why, do you fancy coming?' I held his gaze, my eyes twinkling.

'What?' he said, smiling back at me.

This was the moment I either pretended I'd been joking, or went through with it and invited him properly. What would it be? I didn't stop to think. 'Do you fancy coming out there?' I said.

He grinned. 'Yeah, I wouldn't mind. What would I have to do to make it happen?'

My heart leapt. 'You'll have to get a passport,' I said, trying to keep my voice steady. It was easy to get a passport then. You just went to the post office with a photo and ten quid and they gave you a temporary folded-up document with your picture and a stamp on it.

I told him the dates of the trip and which airline we were flying with. 'I won't be long,' he said, making his way out of the pub. He came back later in the afternoon. 'I've got my fare and I've got my passport,' he said. 'Can my mate Tony come?'

I couldn't see why not. I didn't think Jan would mind. 'Yeah, all right,' I said.

Me and Jan flew out there a couple of days before they did. We met them at the airport and it was great from the moment they arrived. Jan and Tony had a right laugh, just as mates, and me and Jimmy had a ball.

What's good for the goose is good for the gander, I thought. Sod you, George, I'm going to do what you're doing. I had always been faithful and completely straight with him, but now I decided that I'd had enough. I felt I deserved a holiday romance.

I quickly found that my feelings for Jimmy were completely different from my feelings for George. It was fireworks and sheer happiness with Jimmy, in and out of bed. It was magic. We had a lovely, lovely time. We knew it wasn't going anywhere. It was just a bit of fun. However, if I'd known how things were going to work out, I might have taken it more seriously.

Just in case he decided to check up on me, I'd told George that we were going to the other side of the island. But Jan's husband knew where we were. So when someone tipped George off that me and Jan weren't alone in Ibiza, he went round to Jan's house to find out exactly where we'd gone. Unbeknown to us, he then flew out to Ibiza to look for me, a couple of days before we were due to come home.

What's funny is that me and Jimmy would see planes going over while we were lying on the beach and joke, 'There's George, flying out to find us!' Little did we know that he really was.

When he landed, George went everywhere he could think of to find us. I'd been to Ibiza with him in previous years, so he knew roughly where we'd be. Embarrassingly, he took a photograph of me around to all the bars and restaurants in the area. He went up to the waiters and people sitting at the tables. 'Have you seen this person?' he demanded. Thankfully, no one let on, even if they had.

Oblivious to it all, me, Jan, Jimmy and Tony went back to the airport. The bloke whose villa it was gave us a lift there. Jimmy and Tony had another three days in Ibiza, but they came to see us off.

As we walked towards the check-in desk, arm in arm, Jan said, 'There's George!'

'What?' I said, with a laugh. I thought she was joking. But then I looked up to where she was pointing and blow me down if George wasn't on the balcony above with a zoom-lens camera trained on us.

'Oh my God!'

George rushed down to our floor and confronted us. There was murders between him and Jimmy and it looked like there was going to be a fight. 'You can't do this here! You'll get locked up!' I said.

That must have made George think twice, because he quickly walked away. Then he called Jan over. 'Did she sleep with him?' he asked her, pointing at Jimmy.

'No, no!' she insisted.

Then he called me over and accused me of going with Jimmy. 'No, we're just friends,' I assured him.

He blustered and argued with me until it was time to get on the plane. I was relieved to be getting away from him until I realised that he had booked himself on the same Iberia flight as me and Jan. They weren't so strict about not revealing flight passenger lists in those days, but he still must have told a load of lies to the airline staff to track our flight.

Twenty minutes later, me, George and Jan were sitting together at the back of the plane, with George firmly seated between me and Jan. He wouldn't let us go to the toilet together, in case we took the chance to collaborate and get our story straight, so it felt a bit like we'd been arrested. We had earache by the time we landed at Heathrow, because he fired accusations at us for two and a half hours.

'No,' I kept saying. 'Nothing happened. Why can't you just accept it?' He went on and on, getting angrier and angrier. I couldn't help wondering why he was getting so hot and bothered. He hadn't been faithful to me for years, so why was he so worried about me going off with someone?

Jan's husband met her at Heathrow. He was as nice as pie. 'We'll come over to you later and have something to eat,' he said. But things didn't work out that way.

George had his car at the airport and insisted on driving me home. But instead of following the signs towards London, we started heading out into the countryside. 'Where are we going?' I asked him. It was getting dark. Fear pricked the back of my neck. Where was he taking me?

'I want to know what's gone on,' he said.

'Nothing went on!' I kept saying it over and over again. 'He's just a friend. We met them out there.'

'You expect me to believe that? I saw you at the airport. I know something went on, you lying cow.'

He turned down a country lane and pulled up. I fell silent, fearful of what was coming next. I was right to be afraid. He punched me in the head, then he punched me again, shouting and yelling, spewing out accusations.

Over the next few hours, he knocked seven bells of shit out of me. He made sure not to hurt my face or give me any black eyes, but he really bashed me up. It was incredibly frightening, because there was no one around to call for help. We were totally alone in the pitch-black night.

He wouldn't stop hitting me. It went on and on. I was wearing a sovereign ring on my middle finger and at one point he squeezed my hand so hard that the coin popped out of the ring shank. 'I know you went with him, you filthy slag! I know you did!' he yelled.

I wanted to say, 'Why are you so bothered about it, anyway? You do it all the time!' But I didn't dare. He'd just say I was imagining it, as he always did. He might also take it as an admission of guilt.

Now and then, he strayed off the subject and accused me of all sorts of random stuff. 'You don't give a monkey's about me. I bet you wouldn't even come to my funeral!' he said.

'You know I don't go to funerals,' I said. 'Anyway, what's that got to do with it?'

'Shut up, you bitch!' he shouted, bashing me again.

After a while, his voice began to sound muffled. Then I could hardly hear him at all. 'Oh my God, George,' I whispered, worried that he'd done some permanent damage. 'I can't hear anything. You'd better take me to hospital.'

Eventually he drove me to Guy's Hospital and dropped me off outside. My head was killing me.

'I was attacked at a bus stop,' I told the doctors. They admitted me straight away. The police were called and I had to make up a whole story about what had happened. Nothing came of it, of course. They'd probably heard that story a million times.

I stayed in hospital for a couple of days. It was terrible. I was in agony most of the time, sobbing with pain and shock. I have to get out of this relationship, I thought. But I knew deep down that George wouldn't let me go.

I rang Jan when I was discharged. She and her husband came and picked me up from Guy's. Blow me down if George wasn't driving by as we came out of the front entrance! I ignored him and got in my friends' car. Jan and her husband took me back to their place and I stayed there while I recovered. I didn't tell anyone George had knocked me about. I told my mum I'd had an accident.

I was scared of George now. He turned nasty after that and hit me again from time to time. I should have left him, but I was too frightened. He went on about Jimmy for a long,

long time and I had to keep saying I hadn't done anything wrong. I didn't see Jimmy again, not to speak to anyway. George said I couldn't work in the pub any more, so I didn't. That was that. 'You ain't seeing that Jan no more, either,' he told me. I still saw her on the quiet, but I had to watch myself. George had a key to the flat, so he could come in any time he wanted to.

I'd had ten days of magic with Jimmy, but that was in the past. I couldn't stop thinking about him, though. I thought of him every time 'Give Me The Night' came on the radio. But I didn't have the confidence to go and knock on his door. What if he sent me away?

My life was much quieter now that I wasn't working in the pub. I spent as much time as I could with Tracy, although I couldn't get over to Battersea as much as I wanted to, because it was so far away. Tracy wasn't just my daughter, she was my mate, and she still is. She's my best mate. She was always older than her years and we got on really well.

I could always tell when she had something on her mind, so when she turned up at my house looking agitated one Sunday, I immediately asked her what was up. 'I'm pregnant, Mum,' she said. I tried to hide my disappointment. She was eighteen years old, the same age I'd been when I gave birth to her.

I didn't want her to have a baby at that age. I didn't want her to turn out like me. But who can say what's right and what's wrong? You can't predict how someone will turn out, and you can't control them.

By then, she had been with her boyfriend for years and years. She'd first met him at the youth club on the

My beloved mum and dad on their wedding day. Far left is Granddad Alf. Far right are 'Uncle Bill' and Nan.

Me and my sister Jackie dressed up at Monson Road Primary School. I was a lion tamer!

Me aged eighteen months.

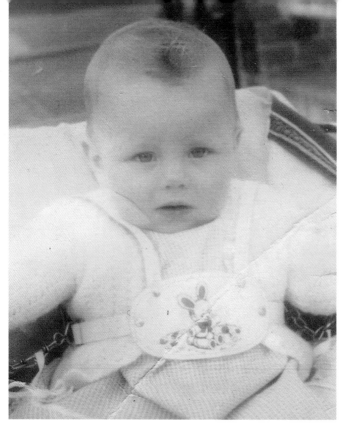

My beautiful daughter Tracy. I was just seventeen when I fell pregnant.

Family is really important to me. Here I am with two of my grandkids, Brooke and Danny, on holiday in Spain.

On the red carpet for Gary's film *Dracula* with (l-r) Mum, Gary and Jackie. I was so proud of my little brother.

Me, Jackie and Mum at Mum's eightieth birthday party, on board the *Queen Mary*.

On my wedding day to 'Ginger Jim'. Isabella Rossellini's behind me in the trouser suit.

On the set of *Nil by Mouth*, the film that changed my life.

With Kathy Burke in *Nil by Mouth*.

A shot from the Christmas Day episode of *EastEnders* in 2005. The 'bird' I'd been promised for the big dinner wasn't quite what I was expecting – much to the disappointment of (l-r) Kat, Alfie, Charlie and Stacey. I never imagined that one day I'd join the cast of *EastEnders* …

… nor meet the Queen – in the Queen Vic! Funny how life turns out. I'm in the middle, waiting my turn to curtsy and say, 'How do you do, Ma'am?'

I made some good friends on *EastEnders* – foremost among them Wendy Richard. Here we are on a night out with Leslie Grantham and my mate Jan. I miss Wendy every day.

Doing *Thriller* for Children in Need in 2003. Blimey! I'm Death-Warmed-Up in the top-right corner.

Singing our hearts out: with June Brown at John Bardon's wedding.

With Matt Damon and Tim Monarch on the set of *The Good Shepherd*.

Life's never seemed brighter.
(inset) With my Jimmy on a
trip to Oxford.

Winstanley Estate in Battersea when she was just eleven. Back then, he'd had thick black hair and wore a leather jacket and jeans. She thought he looked like the Fonz. Yeah, I like him! she decided. It wasn't long before they started going out. Everybody fancied him and so she was the lucky one. Or that's how it seemed in the beginning.

He was the only boyfriend Tracy ever had. They grew up together and stayed together. I always liked him, even when he went through his punk rocker stage around 1977. He used to buy his clothes and bondage gear in the Vivienne Westwood shop on the King's Road, and he went to all the punk gigs around London. He had his hair sticking up and wore those trousers with elastic across them and safety pins all up them. To me, they looked like napkins!

I used to look at him and think, Oh my God! I was grateful that Tracy wasn't into dressing up like that. She didn't go with him to the gigs, either, although she did see Siouxsie and the Banshees when they came and played at the Winstanley Youth Club, before they made it big.

I often recognised myself in Tracy. Like me, she never liked school. Like me, she started bunking off when she was about twelve. I understood, but as a parent I had to be strict. When the school wrote to me and told me she'd been playing truant, I walloped her with the plastic spatula.

Tracy found George very strict. She wasn't a fan of his as she grew up, because she didn't like to be told what to do. He was looking out for her, but that's not the way she saw it.

'Can I go to my friend's party tonight?' she asked, one morning.

'Yeah, if you're in by half ten,' George said.

'But it starts at half ten!' she whined.

'Oh well, forget it, then. You can't go.' I had to agree with him. She was only fourteen at the time. I couldn't allow her to stay out half the night.

Later that day, she tried one of my old tricks, without knowing it. She rang up and said, 'I'm going to stay at Nicola's tonight.'

George wasn't having any of it. 'I don't believe for one minute that she's staying at Nicola's house,' he said. Neither did I. After all, hadn't I been the same?

George and I went round to Nicola's house. 'Isn't Nicola staying at your house?' her mum said. I couldn't help laughing. It was me and Jennifer Crew all over again!

When we explained the situation to Nicola's mum, she rang someone who rang someone else and eventually we found out the address of the party. Poor Tracy! She was mortified when we turned up, marched in and dragged her out of there. Even worse, I punished her by keeping her in for six weeks. She nearly went mad with frustration!

Tracy left school at fifteen. She worked in Sainsbury's for a while and then she got a job in the offices of a computer company in Borough, near London Bridge. She loved it there. But now she was pregnant and the job had to end. It felt like history was repeating itself. I was upset about it, but I really hoped that she'd be happy.

Danny arrived in 1983. Tracy had a terrible birth. I was at the hospital with her, but I was too squeamish to go into the delivery room, so my sister Jackie stayed with her. She was twenty hours in labour and in the end they used a ventouse to get the baby out, all seven pounds, eleven ounces of him. Bully Beef! But it was worth it. Danny was a lovely baby and he grew up to be a very handsome boy. I think he looks like Tom Cruise now he's grown up, but Tracy's friend says he's more like Leonardo di Caprio. You get the picture: he's good looking.

I really hoped Tracy would enjoy family life: a new bonny baby and a handsome bloke, and her childhood sweetheart at that – all the happiness you could hope for. But it didn't turn out like that.

I was devastated for my daughter when I realised there was violence in her relationship. I wanted to protect my little girl so much. Yet there was nothing I could do. She loved him. She wasn't going to leave him. All I could do was try to be there for her, whenever she needed me.

I tried to be there for both my kids. Gerry came home from boarding school when he was nearly fifteen. I was really happy to have my boy back with me, especially as he seemed a lot better behaved than he'd been before he went away. He was glad to be home and, for a few weeks, I thought the school had done its job and calmed him right down.

But then he fell in with the wrong crowd and he was soon in trouble again. It was his personality; he was too easily led. It was a nightmare getting him to school and then I'd get regular phone calls saying that he had run out of the gates.

At least he had learned to read and write by then, though. They taught him to write beautifully in Yeovil.

He wasn't glue sniffing any more – but he'd started puffing marijuana. From there, he experimented with heroin, and inevitably he became addicted. It wasn't long before he was injecting it and stealing to feed his habit.

The police were always ringing up to say, 'We've got your boy here.' It felt like I was constantly up at the police station, or having to bail him out or go to court. Finally, just before he turned sixteen, he was sent to a borstal in Kent, for thieving. The worst of it was that it felt sadly predictable, despite everything I'd tried to do to stop it happening. But it wasn't enough.

I've always loved Gerry, always cared deeply for him. He was a lovely boy in so many ways: when he wasn't being naughty, he was funny, loving and sweet. I used to say, 'You're not getting a penny off me! You're getting nothing off me,' but I often landed up giving him money. I'd leave £20 under the mat, or slip him a note here and there. I wasn't helping him by giving him money; I did it to stop him from robbing someone, or breaking in somewhere, which would inevitably lead to him being nicked and sent away. It was like being caught between the devil and the deep blue sea. It made no difference what I did, though. He was put away, he came out, he was put on probation and he was put away again. The cycle just kept repeating.

It's nasty going to visit your son in prison. I always dreaded it. Prisons are such grim, desolate places and I hated to see Gerry locked up. It was the same routine every time I went to see him.

First, I'd sit in a waiting room with all the other visitors. Sometimes I'd have a chat with another prisoner's mother or relative: 'Blimmin' journey, this is!' I'd find out how they were getting home and offer them a lift, or drop them at the nearest station. Since I was always in the car, it was nice to be able to help out.

After waiting around for a bit, we'd go through a security check, similar to the airport checks they do now. All our bags and bits and pieces had to go into a lock-up, including all paper money. We were only allowed to take change in with us and they frisked us to make sure we weren't hiding weapons or drugs.

Then we'd be shown into a big hall, where we'd sit at different tables and wait for the prisoners to be brought in. Oh, it was awful. Gerry was always upset when he saw me, and I'd come out just crying my eyes out.

But at least he's safe, I'd think to myself. It was my one consolation. While he was away, he couldn't get up to anything bad, or get killed. My heart wouldn't constantly be in my mouth, worrying that the police would come knocking. In that way, at least, it was a relief to know where he was and that he was all right.

Every time he was sent away, he would say, 'Mum, you're always right. Why don't I listen to you?'

'Because you get involved with people that are no good,' I'd say. 'They talk you into taking this or doing that and you do it. Then they get away and you get caught. It happens every time.'

The way I see it, if you're going to be bad, don't get caught. Stay under the radar. But drug addicts are unpredictable and uncontrollable. It's like a demon enters them and they don't fully know what they're doing. I had so much stuff go missing over the years. I used to hide my valuables, my bag and my purse, because Gerry would take anything he could find just to get a £10 bag of gear, even if what he'd nicked was actually worth £300. He was endlessly chasing the next bit of stuff.

My mum wouldn't have him at her house. 'He ain't staying here,' she'd say.

Sometimes when I was at Mum's I'd hear a pebble against the window in the early hours of the morning. I'd open the window and whisper, 'Be quiet!' Then I'd creep downstairs and let him in. He'd lie down by the side of my bed, hidden from view, until the next morning, when we'd wait for Mum to go out shopping before he could leave the house. To this day, Mum doesn't know I did that!

As time went on, Gerry spent more time locked away, until it seemed like he was always in a borstal or prison. After Kent he was sent to a borstal in Rochester, and after that a Young Offender Institution in Hertfordshire, which was for boys aged between eighteen and twenty-one. When he was nineteen, he went to High Down Prison in Surrey; later to Weyland Prison in Norfolk. He's also been to Belmarsh and Brixton over the years. Sad as it is to say, I've lost count of the number of times he's been away now.

He never hurt anybody. He was just a thief. That's what he did. He nicked, took drugs, went to prison, came out and did the same thing all over again. There was nothing I could do to stop him. I lost control of him the day he inhaled his first bag of Bostik.

But I never stopped loving him, not for a single moment.

chapter eight

Sliding Doors

I OFTEN THOUGHT about Dad. I hadn't seen him for many years, but I still missed him all the time. I couldn't help wishing that one day the phone would ring and it would be him, or I'd answer the door and find him on the doorstep. But it didn't happen.

I knew Mum was in contact with Dad from time to time, but she didn't really talk about it and I didn't like to ask. I didn't want to pry into her life, in the same way that I didn't want anybody to pry into mine. All she ever said was that Dad was fine and living in the caravan park with Pat, who was still confined to a wheelchair.

Mum had remarried about six years after Dad left, but it was a marriage of companionship, nothing more. Although she and her second husband Patrick got on really well, they never indulged in a physical relationship. She looked after him when he became ill and was very sad when he died, four years after they got married. She wasn't devastated, though. She's been on her own ever since.

My father was the big love of her life and I don't think she ever stopped loving him. She certainly forgave him. One day in 1983, out of the blue, she said, 'Your dad's invited us down to see him for the day. I'm going a week on Saturday. Would you like to come?'

I didn't hesitate for a second. 'Yes,' I said. 'I'll bring Gerry.' Dad and my boy had never met, because Dad left before

Gerry was born. Gerry was in his mid-teens at that time; it was just after he'd come back from boarding school.

I drove us down to Canterbury. We took Gerry and Sally Ann, Jackie's youngest daughter. As we drew near, I began to feel nervous. I kept thinking about the last time I'd seen Dad, when I'd gone down with George and he had sent me away. I had to keep reminding myself that this time he had invited us. He knew I was coming.

I was longing to see him and desperately hoping for a smile and a hug from him. I needed to know that he loved me, and I wanted him to know that I still loved him, every bit as much as I always had.

Dad met us at the gates of the caravan park. I knew it was him immediately, but I was shocked by how much he had aged. His hair was white and he looked like an old man, even though he was only sixty-two. He was still Dad, though. He had the same humorous face and twinkly eyes; he still made us laugh. He seemed happy, but I couldn't help wondering if he sometimes wished he'd never left my mum. When Pat became ill, no one could have blamed him for thinking, What a bloody big mistake I've made!

We had lunch at the local pub and then went to a big park, where the kids could play. Sally Ann and Gerry ran off to climb trees while me and Mum talked to Dad. When Dad put his arm round me and gave me a cuddle, I felt happier than I had in a long time. We reminisced a little and laughed about things we'd seen and done together, years before. There was no bad feeling between us, only love and forgiveness. It was even better than I'd hoped it would be.

I went off for a while so Mum could talk to Dad alone. I don't know what they spoke about, but I think he must have said sorry to her. She didn't let on and I didn't ask. I didn't need to know. It was enough to see Dad again and feel loved by him, and to show him how much I loved him.

Gary was still away doing his own thing. After he graduated from drama college, he went off doing theatre around the country, from London to Glasgow and back again. In 1982, he appeared in his first film, *Remembrance*, and the following year he played a skinhead in Mike Leigh's film, *Meantime*. Then he did more theatre. He always seemed to be working. He mixed in totally different circles to me, with actors and arty people.

'Your Gary's getting on well,' people started saying to me. 'You must be pleased.'

"Course I am! He's my brother.'

We didn't see much of him, but he rang my mum to tell her what he was up to and she'd pass on all his news. 'Oh, lovely!' we'd say, when we heard he had a new play on, or he'd been picked for a film. We were very proud of him. Me, Jackie and Mum went to see him in a couple of plays at the Royal Court Theatre in London and it was clear that he was really good at what he did, and he was very dedicated to it. We were all sure he'd do well, although we didn't expect him to become a star living out in Hollywood!

George and Gary didn't really know each other, because I mostly saw Gary at Mum's, and at family get-togethers. He and George were a bit like ships in the night and hardly ever met. I wasn't seeing much of George now, anyway. He came and went as he pleased and I tried not to sit around waiting for him. I wasn't happy about it, but I didn't talk to anyone. I tend not to confide in people. I prefer to keep things to myself.

I had stopped threatening to leave George years before. If I even mentioned that we'd be better off without each other, he would turn nasty and accuse me of seeing someone else, so I didn't bother. He was fiercely possessive, yet I hardly saw him. I couldn't really understand what he wanted from me. We kept plodding along. Nothing changed. I was in a rut and I couldn't see how I could get out of it. I was about to find out, though.

Early in 1986, George turned up at the flat with a long face.

'What's up with you?' I asked.

He shifted from one foot to the other. 'There's no easy way to say this, so I'll just get on with it,' he said. 'I've met someone else.'

'You what?' I couldn't believe my ears. We'd had seventeen years together, and for the last ten years I had been trapped in the relationship while he went off with other women. He had kept me on a short leash, beaten me up in jealous rages and accused me of all sorts. Now *he* was leaving *me*?

He shrugged. 'It's over,' he said. He looked uncomfortable. I could tell he wanted to get going.

'I see,' I said, struggling to keep a rein on my feelings. 'That's it, then. No point you hanging around to say anything else. You'd better go.'

On his way out, he hesitated for a moment. 'Mo, I just wanted to say...'

I interrupted him. 'Get lost, George,' I said. 'God will pay you back in a big way for how you've treated me.'

After he left, I poured myself a large vodka and sat down on the sofa. I was in a state of shock. I didn't know whether to laugh or cry. A part of me was devastated, absolutely shattered. I was forty-one years old and after our initial happy years I'd spent the best part of the last decade putting up with someone treating me like dirt. Silly, really, when you look back on it. In all, it was seventeen years down the drain, with nothing to show for it. Why did I stay with him for all those years, when I knew he was a playboy? It was a question I constantly asked myself.

'You ain't leaving me,' he used to say. But when he found someone else, someone permanent, it was a different story.

I wanted to kick myself. I should have ended it after the first seven years, when he'd started to stray. I should have known that it wasn't going to get any better. Then I would have been single again, at thirty-one, with new horizons ahead of me, a whole new world of opportunity. It felt like that movie, *Sliding Doors*. Who knows what life might have opened up to me if I'd had the courage to leave George years before? I might have met someone really nice and settled down properly, instead of having a part-time playboy boyfriend who lied to me more than he told the truth. Or I might have got together with Jimmy and had more than just a holiday romance.

I had often thought about Jimmy over the years, when I heard 'our' song on the radio or saw a film that had been out around the time we'd been in Ibiza. Once, I drove past him walking down the street. I immediately turned the car round, my heart beating wildly, but he was gone by the time I'd driven back to where I'd seen him. What would have happened if I'd had the chance to talk to him? Would the connection still have been there? Would I have left George for him?

Anyway, it didn't happen. I stayed with George, in a half-relationship that made me unhappy for all those years.

Why hadn't I left? At the time, I didn't think I had a choice, but I should have forced the issue. I went over it again and again in my head, driving myself mad. Stop it! I told myself sternly.

There was nothing to be gained from regrets and, anyway, I was glad to be a free agent again, at last – however it had come about. I was relieved that I didn't have to lie to George any more: I didn't need to pretend I hadn't seen Jan or been down the pub with mates. I could do what I wanted without being questioned by someone who was always trying to catch me out. Basically, I didn't have to be scared of George any longer. That was something to celebrate. He had set me free.

I didn't see George again, but a few months after we split up, I bumped into a few of his mates. They knew we'd finished. 'He's always been a playboy,' they told me, as if it was news.

'Isn't it funny how people only tell you what someone is like when the relationship has ended?' I said wryly. 'But I knew what he was like, so you're not telling me anything I didn't already know.'

So George went his way and I went mine. I moved out of the flat in Bowman House and went back to live with my mum. With Gerry away in prison so much and Tracy in her own place with the baby, it wasn't like I really needed my own flat any more. It was better company to be with Mum, anyway. By then, Mum had done a house swap with my sister, taking Jackie's flat in Ilderton Road in New Cross, while Jackie took Mum's house in Hatcham Park Road, just a bit further along off the New Cross Road. It made sense, because Jackie was living with her partner and his two kids, whereas Mum was on her own.

I loved living with Mum. I'd go to work and at the end of the day she'd do me a lovely dinner. She always cooked for me. It was great being looked after and it was a nice, cosy flat. It took me a few months to get over the end of the relationship with George and then I was happier than I'd been in ages.

As it happens, 1986 is a year I'll never forget. It was a year of big events in my life, and most of them weren't pleasant. First, George left, which was a big shock, even though I had mixed emotions about it. Then one of Pat's kids rang Mum, to say that Dad was in hospital with advanced cirrhosis of the liver. 'It sounds like he's dying,' Mum said, ashen-faced.

I was desperately upset. Dad had been such a strong, athletic man when I was a child, always laughing, full of energy and humour. I loved him more than words can express. Despite all the pain he had caused us, I felt incredibly sorry for him. I couldn't help thinking that life had gone downhill for him when he'd left our family. I hated to think of him lying in a hospital bed now, his life ebbing away.

Jackie went down to see him a couple of times, but I couldn't face it and Gary didn't go either. I really hate going to hospitals and seeing people ill; I couldn't bear to see Dad like that. Anyway, Dad and I had already made our peace and said we loved each other. I felt I didn't need to see him again. We had said all there was to say and I much preferred to remember the good times. I know he would have understood.

Dad died in the hospital. He was sixty-five. I've never been one for funerals; I hate the very idea of them. But this was my dad. I had to go.

His funeral was held at a church in Canterbury, on a cold, sunny day. I think Pat's children must have organised it. Pat wasn't there and I don't remember seeing her children; I wouldn't have known what they looked like, anyway. It was a terrible day, so sad and bleak. Thinking about it makes me cry. 'Clair de Lune' by Debussy was playing as Dad's coffin disappeared from view. I don't know why it was played or who thought of it, but it's a beautiful piece of music and it still fetches tears to my eyes when I hear it. There weren't many people at the funeral. I stood in the church with Gary, Mum and Jackie; we listened, said a few prayers and wept. That was it. We drove straight home afterwards.

'I'm never going to another funeral again in my life,' I said, and I've only ever made one exception.

The year 1986 was a difficult one for me, but it was also the year my little brother became a film star, which was amazing and brilliant. Suddenly Gary Oldman was a big name. In his first starring role in a major film, he played the part of Sid Vicious in *Sid And Nancy*, which was about the tragic relationship between the Sex Pistols' bassist and his American girlfriend Nancy Spungen, played by Chloe Webb. Gary's performance won him the *Evening Standard* British Film Award for Most Promising Newcomer. After that, nothing could stop him.

The following year, he played Joe Orton in *Prick Up Your Ears*, another biopic about another destructive relationship, and this time he was nominated for a BAFTA. I thought he was excellent as Joe Orton. Me, Mum and Jackie were so proud of him. Critics started calling him things like 'the best

British actor of his generation' and off he went to America to make his name internationally.

In 1987, he married his first wife, the actor Lesley Manville, and we all went to his wedding, which was a lovely, happy day. Me and Jackie were really pleased for him, although we couldn't help thinking how funny it was to see our baby brother all grown up. They had a son, Alfie, but then the marriage broke down and they went on to divorce. After that, we didn't see Gary much, because he settled in America and didn't come to London very often. When we did meet up, we were the same close-knit family that we'd always been, but it wasn't often that we were all together. Everyone got on with their own lives. Things were good, but sometimes I felt a bit restless. I hadn't met anyone else after George. Tracy was settled and living over in Battersea; I only saw her occasional weekends. Gerry was in prison again. I trundled on in my job.

One night, I rang Gary. He was in South Carolina, working on *Chattahoochee*, with Dennis Hopper and Frances McDormand. 'It's been ages,' I said. 'All right to come and see you?'

"Course it is,' he said.

It was late autumn and very cold when I arrived in South Carolina. I was driven through a vast, lonely landscape to reach the set. I'd never seen anything like it. We were in the middle of nowhere and it was very quiet, but it was incredibly exciting for me. It was my first time on the set of a film and I loved it. I was over the moon when the production manager gave me the job of holding the boom for a couple of days. I had to pinch myself as I climbed the ladder above the set and looked down on the cameras, the backdrops, the crew and actors. Was I really here, operating the boom, with a bird's eye view of the set of a Hollywood film? I could hardly believe it.

Being on set was one thing, spending time with a household name like Dennis Hopper was even more exhilarating. Dennis Hopper, the star of *Easy Rider*! I found him to be a really nice man. By then, he was in his fifties and the nutty days were long behind him. 'Come on, Mogsy!' he'd say with a deep chuckle, picking up on the family nickname for me. 'Let's go eat.'

It was in South Carolina that I first ate sashimi and it's been my favourite food ever since. 'How can you eat raw fish?' people ask me, screwing their faces up in disgust. They're missing out! It's so delicious. I love it.

The next time I went out to America, Gary was in New York, working on a film called *State of Grace* with Sean Penn. He was doing very well by then; he'd already made *Criminal Law* with Kevin Bacon.

'Come and see me, Mogs,' he said, when I rang him. I leapt at the chance.

I went on my own and he met me at the airport. It was really nice to see him again. I stayed at his place overlooking Central Park, not far from Fifth Avenue. He had a beautiful big house with loads of rooms. It was like being in another world, especially as it was my first time in New York. It was breathtaking to see all the tall buildings and lights. I loved it.

South Carolina had been a bit of a whirlwind trip, but this time I stayed a month. We went to parties; we went out to dinner; we visited a lot of people. It was like living in a fairy tale. The Manhattan restaurants were amazing. One of my favourites was the Odeon, which was open until the early hours of the morning. They did beautiful creamed potatoes there. The Russian Tea Rooms was another great place and we went to lots of fantastic sushi restaurants. Everyone I met was warm and approachable. Gary had just started seeing Uma Thurman, whom he later married. She was lovely. I really liked her. She was half my age but we got on really well. In fact, me and Uma mooched about Greenwich Village together on more than one occasion.

I was on the set of *State of Grace* quite a lot, which was really interesting. I love the atmosphere of a film set. There's always so much going on. If we weren't on set, we'd go out, go to a movie, or I went off on my own, round the shops. There were a lot of dollars to your pound back then.

Gary was very generous with me. 'Here you are. Here's a couple of hundred dollars,' he'd say. 'Go and treat yourself.'

Sometimes Gary would go out with his friends and I'd sit in and watch American telly, which I found fascinating. There would be five minutes of telly and ten minutes of adverts! It was enough to put you off switching on. I didn't care, though, because even the commercials were interesting. They were so different from anything you saw on English telly.

It was Sean Penn's birthday while I was there and he had a party in his apartment. It was just the most incredible night for me. Al Pacino was there. Robert De Niro, Christopher Walken, Liza Minnelli, Shelley Winters and Harvey Keitel were there. I was in awe of everyone. I felt very shy and didn't say much. I just looked on and watched it all, dumbstruck.

'This is my sister,' Gary kept saying.

'Hello, how are you?' they all said. 'Pleased to meet you.' Everyone was friendly.

At one point I sat down with a drink and thought, Oh my God! If people in London could see me now with all these stars! When I look back, I wish I'd had a camera with me, although I don't expect I would have dared to take any pictures if I had!

It was a real downer coming back to London. Of course it was. But I got on with it. I was still driving, although now I was delivering car parts and car spares for Mobat's and Canon's. I quite enjoyed my work. I usually had a mate in my van with me, even though I wasn't supposed to have passengers.

A few months later, Uma rang me to say that she was filming *Henry and June* in Paris, while Gary was filming something else in America. Would I like to go out there and see her? she asked. Of course I would! She was cool.

She was a beautiful film star, but I knew her as my sister-in-law and we had a great week together. Most days, we'd go out to eat and shop, then come back and play backgammon. Once we played backgammon from ten in the morning until midnight, stopping only to cook scrambled egg and bacon. We loved it so much! Later, when she came to London, she'd come over to New Cross and we'd go round the corner and have something to eat in the kebab house. I don't think people realised who she was back then, so there was never any unwanted attention. We had some great times.

Hanging out with film stars didn't happen often, though. I was much more likely to be found sitting outside some dingy address in a run-down back street, waiting around for my son. Gerry was in and out of prison as usual, but when he was out, he was still taking drugs and getting into trouble. You never knew what was going to happen from one day to another with him. I always seemed to be running around after him, or with him. I took him here, I took him there, I took him everywhere.

He'd ring me up and say, 'I need to get round the dealer's to take some gear. Will you drive me?'

I couldn't say no to my Gerry. So I'd be going round all these dealers' houses. I'd park around the corner and he'd go in while I waited. It was always tense, waiting outside a dealer's house. God, how I did it, I'll never know! I couldn't do it now. I suppose I thought I was helping him, or I wouldn't have done it. Sometimes I'd do it just to make the problem go away for a few hours, even though I knew the same thing would happen again later, or tomorrow. If I said I was busy, he'd still pester me. He wouldn't take no for an answer and he could always get round me. I hated to see him in agony, desperate for his next fix, but more than that I just didn't want him going out nicking, only to be caught and put away.

Gerry's a complex person. Over the years, he has slept all over the place. He used to squat a lot and he always made his squats lovely. 'Come up and look at my new place, Mum,' he'd say. It would be immaculate. He can't stand dirt; he's always been clean and tidy, which is interesting when you consider his lifestyle.

He lived at Tracy's flat on and off, staying with her and her bloke. He's slept in cars; he stayed in Cardboard City for a long time. He'd sometimes sleep in the garage below Mum's block of flats in Ilderton Road. I used to sneak him down cigarettes, candles and a flask of tea, going in and out when no one was looking. I used to make him up sandwiches and give him biscuits. Oh God, the things I've done! He even slept in the back of my van.

'Shh! Keep your voice down. Don't let your nan hear you,' I'd say, when he rang our buzzer.

Mum was a little better to him after a while. She used to let him come up and have his tea, have a bath and change his clothes. She didn't know he was down in the garage, though!

I'd say, 'I'll see you later, Gel!'

'Yeah, all right.'

'Here's a bit of tobacco. Mind how you go.' We'd pretend he was going off to stay with a friend, but he was only going downstairs!

I could never say no to him. Perhaps if I'd said no a long time ago, he might have changed. On the other hand, he might be dead and I'd have that on my conscience all my life. People say I shouldn't feel guilty, because I'm not responsible for what he does. But it would be on my conscience. I know how I'd feel. I'd think, if I'd have only helped him, it wouldn't have happened … That would have stayed with me, and I couldn't have lived with myself.

He went into several rehabs. Gary put him in two; I put him in at least two. Each time he came out clean, with good intentions, and then went back to the drugs. He was always stealing to buy drugs, although it was mostly just opportunistic nicking. He didn't plan it. His life was too chaotic for that. For instance, one time, he walked past an open door and saw a handbag on the stairs. He took it and the next thing he knew, a geezer came running out of the open door after him. Gerry ran up the road, slipped into a launderette and made the owner lock the door while he scarpered out the back. Only, unfortunately for Gerry, it turned out that there was no way out the back! That was that. He was nicked and put away.

When you're into heroin, it takes hold of you. From what I've seen, you stay hooked until you get to an age when you make a firm decision not to do it any more. That time hasn't come yet for my boy, sadly. The only consolation is that he's never hurt anybody. Whatever he's stolen and whoever he's stolen from, he's never hit anybody doing it. He's never mugged anybody. And when he's sober, Gerry is the nicest, most loving person anybody could wish to meet. He'd do anything for you; he'd run to the ends of the earth.

So many people have said to me, 'Your son's absolutely lovely: so polite, a gentleman.'

I still call him my boy, even though he's a man now. I suppose I'll always be there for him, as I am for both my kids, and the generation after that. Who knows how any of them are going to turn out in later years? No one does. You can be strict as a parent, or lenient, but when your kids grow up, no one knows how they'll turn out. It's the sliding doors again: you don't know which road they will take. People brought up in horrible environments can turn out to be lovely people, refusing outright to be like their parents. And so it goes the other way around. Myra Hindley, Ian Brady: their parents were probably nice people, but they gave birth to monsters. Who knows what someone will do? You can't predict that your child will end up killing someone.

Gerry's antics have been going on for thirty-odd years now. 'How could you have gone through all of that?' people ask. But you just do. When you love your kids, you'd do anything for them.

Some parents get to a point where they say, 'Enough is enough,' and they stop bothering, but I'm not made that way.

My sister says to me, 'How you put up with this, I'll never know.'

'You're just lucky that your two girls have never ventured down that path,' I tell her.

In my opinion, Gerry's bad luck is that he has an addictive nature and is in with the wrong people. I think a big part of it is who you meet and mix with. If you're weak-natured, you cannot mix with people on drugs or boozing. You have to stay well away from them. 'It's only a little bit, it won't hurt ya,' they say. Then you're back on it, hooked again.

Why can't Gerry say, 'No, I'm not having it,' and stay off it? I've never been able to understand it, because I'm not weak in that way. If I say no, I mean no. No one could tempt me to have another drink if I didn't want one. That's the way I am.

I just wish Gerry had taken after me.

chapter nine

Foreign Travels

'HOW D'YOU GET that?' I asked Tracy. She had a nasty black eye again. But she didn't need to tell me how; I knew only too well.

I was just as worried about Tracy as I was about Gerry. By 1990, things were getting out of hand in her relationship. She needed to get away from the violence before she got seriously hurt – but that was easier said than done.

'You want to grab a frying pan and whack him over the head with it,' I suggested.

'That's rich, coming from you!' she replied bitterly. 'You never had the guts to hit back at George!'

She was right. I'd never stood up to George, and I should have done. You forget that when you're trapped in a threatening or violent relationship, you spend a lot of your time on tenterhooks, living in fear. The pressure is intense. When things kick off, your instinct is to minimise the damage, to protect yourself and keep the kids from witnessing the violence. You don't dare risk escalating the situation by hitting back – and anyway, you're scared.

Tracy grew used to being treated badly, I suppose. Still, I knew deep down that she wouldn't stay with him. She was just waiting for the right time to go. 'Leave him now!' I'd urge. It hurt me to see her so unhappy. 'You're mad to stay. You'll find somewhere else to live.'

'I more than likely will, one day,' she'd say.

But when you're frightened of someone, it's not that easy to get away. She kept leaving him and going back. She went to several women's refuges; she came to me; she must have left him five or six times, but she'd always return in the end. Leaving him meant leaving the area and all her friends. It was always going to be a huge wrench for her.

And it was no picnic out in the world. While she was staying at a refuge in Chiswick, for example, one of the other girls stole all of her's and Danny's clothes. Gary gave her £500 to replace them, but she felt she couldn't stay on at the refuge. Inevitably, she went back to her partner. Better the devil you know...

The violence calmed down when Brooke came along in 1992, a young sister for Danny, who was nine by then. Right from the start, I felt a very strong connection with my first granddaughter. It wasn't anything in particular that I could pinpoint, but perhaps she reminded me of me, in some way. Petite and pretty like Tracy, with a sweet, cheeky personality, Brooke was the apple of my eye and I adored her. I often went over to Battersea to pick her up and take her back to Mum's for the weekend. Danny was mad about football and was always off training or playing with his mates, but Brooke came everywhere with me, to the shops, to see friends, out to dinner. From an early age, she was very adventurous with food. She loved her chilli and spices and exotic dishes, which was unusual in someone so young.

The same year Brooke was born, Gary flew me, Jackie and my mum out to Los Angeles for the premiere of *Dracula*. Directed by Francis Ford Coppola, *Dracula* is one of my favourites of Gary's films. He was so good in it. His performance in the title role blew me away. I wasn't intimidated by his success, though. He was my brother, this was his job and he was really good at it; it was as simple as that. I would have been equally impressed if he'd become a brain surgeon. Still, sometimes it was hard to believe that he had achieved so much. And it was amazing to see the rewards and benefits that came with doing so well.

We flew to LA first class on American Airlines. Gary picked us up in a chauffeur-driven car and took us to the Sunset Marquis Hotel, just off Sunset Boulevard, where we stayed for two weeks. It was fabulous there, absolutely stunning. We had a really lovely time. Mum had a room in the hotel and me and Jackie were in a massive villa out the back, which had a huge grand piano in it and overlooked a swimming pool shaded by white canopies. The bathroom was as big as my kitchen at home, with a jet shower. The beds were enormous. It was just amazing to be there; it was like going into Santa's grotto, or Aladdin's cave.

'Isn't it great?' Gary said.

'Aren't we lucky!' I laughed.

We were picked up in a limo to go to the premiere. We felt like royalty. We were all wearing black with a touch of red, to fit the theme of the film. Me and Jackie had bought our dresses in the West End and we looked lovely. At the after-party, we met Winona Ryder, Sadie Frost, Peter Boyle and loads of other actors; we ate sushi and drank champagne. When we left, we were given goodie bags full of make-up. It was all such a treat.

Gary came round to see us every day. We went to Universal Studios and explored Hollywood. It was cracking. The food was lovely: great big Caesar salads, enormous prawns, incredible cheesecakes, Ben & Jerry's ice cream –

even the sandwiches were amazing. The shops were beautiful. Everything was so different. We walked around this magical world in a state of awe.

I loved the film so much that it inspired me to have my first tattoo. I thought it would be unusual to have 'Dracula' written on my foot, so that's what I went for. Gary laughed when he saw it. 'What does it mean?' people often ask. It means I turn into a bat of a nighttime and fly out of the window, of course!

While we were in LA, Gary mentioned that he was thinking about writing and directing his own film. He wanted to produce something very personal, he said. He had all kinds of memories stored up of what he had seen as a kid and a teenager, but more than that, he was inspired to write about life in London – the real stuff, the dark side, that he'd known and seen and witnessed over the years. Well, I knew all about that; God only knew. I thought it sounded great. I really hoped he could pull it off. Slowly but surely, the script of *Nil by Mouth* began to develop.

Around this time, I gave up driving and got a job as a cashier in a betting shop, Coral's in Catford. I enjoyed working there. I got on well with my manager, Paul, and I liked the excitement that every day brought. There's always a drama when people are gambling. I witnessed loads of rows and arguments.

We worked seasonal shifts: in summer, we'd stay late; in winter we'd go home early. I usually arrived before everyone else and got everything ready. I'd lay out the papers, tidy up and open the till. When Paul came in, we'd have a coffee and he'd get all the bets ready. I generally worked on the till or on the payout counter.

The other people in the shop were really nice – and so were the punters, most of the time. Tensions and tempers inevitably ran high, though. Sometimes when I was on the payout, people would come in, slap their ticket down and declare, 'That's wrong!'

'I'm the cashier, not the manager. I don't work the bets out,' I'd say. 'Come back when he's here.'

I had murders. Some people were so rude to me that I'd run outside after them and shout, 'You ain't talking to me like that! I don't care who you are.' It was certainly never dull.

Mum started spending more time out in America with Gary. I flew to New York with her to see him in 1994, while he was taking a break from filming *The Scarlet Letter* with Demi Moore and Robert Duvall in Nova Scotia in the wilds of Canada. It was my second time in New York and I loved it every bit as much as the first. It was always very exciting going to see Gary, it was like escaping into a fantasy world. Again, we went to some fantastic restaurants. Without a doubt, the best food I've eaten has been in New York. Nowhere else comes close.

One evening, me, Mum and Gary were having dinner at Mr Chow, a really top Chinese restaurant, when Gary had a phone call. 'Oh,' he said, when he'd put the phone down. 'I've got to go back to work. You'd better come with me to Nova Scotia.'

That's what I loved about seeing him. You never knew what was going to happen next or where you'd end up! We went back to our hotel and packed our bags. A car came to collect us and took us to the airport, where we got on a small private jet, a six-seater propeller plane. I'm not a nervous flyer, but I remember thinking how small it looked compared to the other planes at the airport.

The pilot's name was Klaus. He spoke with a very deep voice. 'Welcome on board,' he boomed. 'I hope you enjoy your flight.'

It was a dark, blowy night. We took off a little bumpily, but soon levelled out once we were up in the air. This isn't too bad, I thought.

Then, all of a sudden, we hit a snowstorm, a proper blizzard. The plane started swinging and bumping around. It was like something out of a plane crash movie. My stomach was swooping, my palms were sweaty. I started to feel really scared. We're never going to get there! I thought. We're going to die.

Klaus's co-pilot was in charge of the drinks. 'Can I have a large vodka?' I asked her.

She gave me an all-American smile, without a trace of fear in it. 'Sure!'

She coolly mixed me a drink and handed it to me. 'Just leave me the bottle!' I croaked. If I was going to die, I didn't want to know about it. I'd much rather go down in a drunken stupor.

Well, do you think I could get drunk? It was the strangest thing. I was knocking back straight Absolut vodka, but nothing was happening. I was so frightened that my body wouldn't let me get drunk. I drank almost the whole bottle, give or take an inch or two, but I stayed sober as a judge. My mind was sharp as a pin. I wasn't even slightly wobbly. It was incredibly frustrating, because I needed anaesthetising. However, the vodka was going in, but my adrenaline was overriding it.

I looked over at Gary. He was sitting calmly with his little sausage dog in a basket on his lap. He didn't seem too worried.

'Are you frightened?' I asked Mum.

'No,' she said.

Don't tell lies, I thought. You are! I can see it. I shut my eyes and tried to think of nice things.

Eventually, we landed safely, with a bump. Thank God for that! I thought.

But the journey was by no means over. Now we had to drive through thick snow to the house where we were staying. It took ages. The driver crawled along, doing about five miles an hour. 'Can't you go any faster?' I politely asked him, silently seething with impatience. After the flight from hell, I just wanted to get there, and I could see that Mum and Gary did too.

Finally, at around three o'clock in the morning, the house came into view. It was an imposing wooden building, like something out of *The Amityville Horror*, lit up in the night, a dramatic sight in the snowy landscape that surrounded it. We pulled up outside, got stiffly out of the car and gratefully walked inside. The house was absolutely beautiful, made entirely of wood and glass, a work of art in its own right. Tired as I was, I couldn't help gulping in awe.

Gary's dialect coach, Tim Monarch, was already there. I had met him several times before. He's a lovely man. We said hello, had a cup of tea and went to bed.

The next day, Gary got up early to go on set, but Mum and I slept in. We had a lovely relaxing time for the next few days: we went to visit Gary on set a couple of times and we also did quite a bit of sightseeing. It was a picturesque area. The countryside was incredible and we visited a couple of beautiful, old-fashioned towns.

One day Gary went off filming and me and Mum stayed at the house. We were in the lounge when I noticed that there was a funny noise coming from somewhere, a dull droning sound. 'I wonder where that noise is coming from, Mum?' I said.

She cocked her head. 'Maybe upstairs?' she suggested.

We walked around a bit, trying to locate its source, then we climbed the wooden stairs to the first floor. Our footsteps echoed on the polished floor. The noise was louder now. 'It's coming from Gary's bedroom,' I said. 'What the hell is it?'

I stood outside his door, listening. An insistent buzzing was coming from inside the room, but for the life of me I couldn't work out what it was. It didn't sound like a machine, but what else could it be?

Bracing myself, I opened the door and walked into the room. The scene that greeted me really was like something out of *The Amityville Horror*. The room was semi-dark, the light blocked out by thousands, maybe millions, of big black sticky flies, which were crawling over the windows and walls in a great teeming, droning mass. Thousands more flies were swarming down from the eaves of the roof in big buzzing clouds. Basically, there were flies everywhere. You could hardly breathe without inhaling them.

Terrified, I ran out of the room and slammed the door. 'Oh my God, Mum!' I yelled. 'The place is infested. What are we going to do?'

In my shock and panic, I decided that this was a problem I needed to solve there and then. I searched my mind for options. I had to move fast before the whole room filled up with insects.

'Get me a Hoover!' I told Mum.

'Where from?' she said.

I was in a right two and eight. 'I don't know! Isn't there a broom cupboard somewhere?'

Eventually, we found a Hoover, a good one, too. I lugged it into Gary's room and turned it on. The plan was to suck up the flies, killing them in the process. But they seemed to be multiplying at a disturbing rate, swarming through the air and landing on the windows as fast as I could vacuum them up. It felt like a nightmare, a supernatural dream. It soon became clear that I'd need at least ten Hoovers to make an impact – and even then, I wasn't sure I'd be able to overcome all the flies.

The sight of them all crawling over each other started to make me feel physically sick. 'It's no good,' I told Mum. 'We'll have to get help.'

Dumping the vacuum cleaner, I ran out of the room, firmly shut the door and rang Gary's assistant for help. Half an hour later, I breathed a sigh of relief as a pest control van drew up outside the house. Why on earth I'd thought that I could singlehandedly overcome a plague of flies, I don't know! After that, the house gave me the creeps. It's really lucky that Gary wasn't there to see his room under attack. He wouldn't have slept in there afterwards if he'd seen what I had.

Apart from that afternoon of horror, Mum and I had a lovely trip to Nova Scotia. We went back to New York when Gary had finished filming and then flew home to London from there.

It was depressing to be back. Gerry was in prison again and things were deteriorating fast in Tracy's relationship. Brooke's arrival had helped temper things for a bit, but the truce hadn't lasted. One day I went round to see her, only to find her in a terrible state. She had a huge gash in her head, a crushed thumb, two black eyes, a carpet burn on her face and massive bruises all over her body. It was the worst I'd ever seen her. I was horrified by her injuries. Her head had ballooned, her face was grotesquely blown up and her cheeks were spongy. She was black and blue.

'Oh my God, what happened to you?' I asked, aghast.

'A car ran me over,' she lisped through swollen, split lips.

'What do you mean, you got run over? Where?'

'Round by the shops,' she said. 'It was a hit and run. He just seemed to come out of nowhere.'

Her injuries were so serious that I believed her. 'Didn't no one see it? Didn't you clock the number plate?' I asked frantically. 'That bastard could have killed you!' Tears were running down my face. I was appalled. Her injuries were shocking. I could hardly bear to look at her.

It was weeks before she told me the truth. 'Oh no,' I said, when she finally came clean about it. I was devastated to think that her partner had done that to her. 'You'll have to leave him. It can't happen again.'

And, incredibly, it didn't. Not long afterwards, she somehow found the strength to stand up to him. She said she woke up one day and just felt different, stronger. I was proud of her. But it was still another four years before she finally got away. Things like that don't just get sorted overnight.

Meanwhile, I was nearing fifty and still living with my mum and working in the betting shop. I wasn't unhappy, but I was bored, and I had a dim view of what the future held for me. I enjoyed seeing my friends, but there was definitely something missing. It felt like my life was going nowhere. I went out with a couple of blokes, but no one to speak of. It didn't take long to realise that none of them were my cup of tea. I usually knew after just one evening out with a bloke that I didn't want to get entangled. Sometimes it took a week or two.

Then, one evening in 1994, I went to the pub with Lesley, Jackie's eldest daughter. A ginger-haired bloke called Jim was in there, propping up the bar. 'Hello, Maureen!' he said, greeting me like a long-lost friend. He was boozed. He had a load of smoked salmon on him. Someone had brought it in to the pub and he'd bought the whole lot from them.

'Who's that?' Lesley asked.

'You don't want to know,' I said dismissively. Over the years, I'd often seen him out, in one pub or another. He was always drunk, always a nuisance. He was the kind of person you wanted to get away from.

'How's your brother?' Jim asked, swaying.

'He's fine, thanks,' I said abruptly.

'I'll take you out one night,' he said, digging into his jacket pocket. 'Here's my card.'

I took it out of politeness. Yeah, I thought, and I left it.

About two weeks later, I was feeling fed up and decided to give him a ring. Perhaps it would be a laugh to go out with him for just one evening, I thought. After all, what had I got to lose?

'Would you like to go out to dinner?' he asked when I rang him.

'All right.'

I met him at the same pub. We had a couple of drinks and he took me out for something to eat. To my complete surprise, I found I enjoyed his company. He seemed all right, a different person to the one I'd known for all those years. He was funny and made me laugh, although he wasn't a looker. I used to call him 'Ginger Jim'.

He might have changed, I thought hopefully. He might not be such a big boozer these days. After all, you have to give someone the benefit of the doubt.

A couple of days later, he asked me up to his flat for tea. 'I'll cook you a dinner,' he said.

'All right.' When I arrived and looked in his fridge, there was beer and nothing else. 'What are you cooking for me, then?' I asked.

He went to the cupboard and took out a tin of beef stew! 'Right, I'll cook next time,' I said.

We went out a few times and then one thing led to another. He wasn't drinking so much then; I suppose he was on his best behaviour. I started staying at his flat overlooking the river in Deptford Wharf. It was a nice place. I could get used to this, I thought.

'I want to marry you!' he said, three weeks later, finishing his last mouthful of the roast dinner I'd just cooked him.

'Only because I'm a good cook,' I said.

'Yeah, I know!' he said, smiling at his empty plate. 'And I love you,' he added. 'I mean it, will you marry me?'

'What?' I screeched. I couldn't help smiling. I didn't love him, but I liked him and maybe my feelings would grow as I got to know him better. 'I'll think about it,' I said. 'If I'm still with you in six months, I might do.'

I married him six months down the line as a way out, a move away from my mum. It meant I could get a dog, which was brilliant, because I love dogs and had always wanted one. My first dog was a dachshund called Sundee. Then I got another dachshund and called him John Lennon, after my favourite Beatle.

My wedding to Jim took place at Lewisham Register

Office in July 1995. It helped that my family liked him, but I never really loved him, not truly and deeply. I told him I did, perhaps because he had a few quid, but the feelings weren't there. Still, it was a lovely day and the weather was gorgeous. We had a hundred guests and all my family were there, including Gary and my mum. Gary came with Isabella Rossellini, who he was dating at the time. I was happy, because I had everybody I loved around me and I was wearing a pretty wedding dress! The reception was at the Spaghetti Western in Dulwich. Ginger Jim paid. It cost about seven grand.

'Congratulations!' people kept saying.

'Thanks!' I replied, hoping against hope that things would work out the second time around.

If I'd known what was about to happen and how much my life was going to change, I'm sure I wouldn't have married him. But how was I to know? I simply didn't have a clue.

chapter ten

A Complete Turnaround

JIMMY TOOK ME to Corfu for our honeymoon. It was beautiful there and we had some fun times, but a couple of things happened that rang warning bells for me. One lunchtime, he got so drunk that he couldn't string a sensible sentence together. He turned into a slurring, repetitive bore and then passed out for the rest of the day. Oh God, I thought. Maybe he hasn't changed after all.

Another time, I found an empty vodka bottle at the back of the wardrobe in our room. 'What's this doing here?' I asked him.

'What is it?' he said, feigning ignorance.

'You know bloody well what it is!' I said sharply. 'What's it doing in the wardrobe?'

'How would I know?' he said, shrugging. He tried to blame it on a past guest.

It wasn't long before I realised that he was still the same old boozer that I'd known over the years. Of course he was. Leopards don't change their spots. He had managed to keep it together for the last six months, but now that he'd put a ring on my finger, he thought he could do what he liked. Sundays were the worst. He'd get so drunk in the pub before dinner that he could hardly hold his knife and fork.

'Why do I go to the bother of cooking you a roast dinner if you get so drunk you don't know where your mouth is?' I'd yell at him. It wound me up so much. We still had good times, but from then on I had a feeling that the marriage wouldn't go the distance.

I was glad when Gary arrived in London to do the prep for *Nil by Mouth* in September. It had taken him a long time to write the script and get the film up and running, but he was now almost ready to go. He set up the film's offices in Deptford. 'If you want, you can be my driver,' he said.

So I packed my job in at the betting shop and drove my old banger over to Deptford. For a few weeks, I drove Gary around on location reccies, or picked up and dropped off members of the cast and crew. It was good fun. Every day was different.

Me and Gary had some interesting times looking for locations. We explored all the cockney haunts and drove down some moody back roads. 'Let's go the back way!' he was always saying. Although he had a location manager, he liked to go and see everywhere himself. Endlessly curious and restless, he's like me in that he can't keep still.

Rehearsals began with the film's main actors. Set on a council estate in south-east London, *Nil by Mouth* is about a working-class family coping with serious difficulties. Val (Kathy Burke) is married to a violent geezer with a coke problem called Ray (Ray Winstone); her brother Billy (Charlie Creed-Miles) is a junkie, always chasing his next bit of gear; Val and Billy's mother, Janet, lives with her old mum (Edna Doré) and does the best she can for her kids. The film builds up to a harrowing scene in which Ray beats pregnant Val black and blue. Afterwards, Val tells Janet that her horrific injuries were caused by a car running her over and Ray explains to his mate Mark (Jamie Foreman) that his father was a vicious alcoholic. At the end of the film, Billy is in prison and it appears that Val has forgiven Ray.

Almost everything in the script has happened to members of my family, in essence. Although the details are not exact, a lot of the scenes are inspired by actual events. The film is not based on anyone's life in particular, but it's a mix-up of events, some of them things that actually happened and others completely invented. And while Gary didn't specifically base any character on any one person, from the start I felt a special connection with Janet, Val and Billy's mother. Everything that happens to Janet has happened to me – and worse. Some elements were different here and there. The dialogue was written by Gary, obviously. But otherwise it was very true to my life.

It was Gary's first time directing, but he seemed to know exactly what he was doing.

'You could be in this,' he said to me one day, early into rehearsals.

'Leave off, I'm not an actress,' I said. I thought nothing more of it.

A few weeks later, it became clear that he wasn't happy with the actress who was playing Janet. She was a very good actor, but the part didn't quite fit.

'This is not going right,' Gary said, as I was driving him back to his hotel. 'I don't know what I'm going to do. I think I'll have to replace her.'

Then there was a pause. I could feel Gary's eyes on me. 'I think you could do this, Mogs,' he said. 'Come back to the hotel and read.'

'Me?' I snapped. 'I'm not doing it! I don't know anything about acting.'

'Just come back with me and read a bit,' he said gently.

So, instead of dropping him off at the hotel, I went up to Gary's room, where he handed me a page of dialogue. 'Have a little look at that,' he said.

'All right.' My eyes darted down the page. It was the first time I'd seen the script, although obviously I knew what it was all about. 'OK.'

Five minutes later, Gary said, 'Go on then, read it.'

'What, now?'

'Yeah.'

The dialogue began with Janet coming out of the toilet.

You don't want to go in there just yet. I think a rat's crawled up my arse and died,' she says.

Janet's daughter calls out, *'Wanna cup of tea, Mum?'*

'Yes please, love. Make it a strong one, none of that sham-rock shit.'

'What's that?' asks Janet's son.

'Three leaves,' she explains.

Her son-in-law makes farting noises, because she's been in the toilet so long. *'Give that cunt a dose of poison!'* she says to her daughter.

That was it. I'd reached the end of the page. I looked over at Gary. He was grinning. 'You're doing this!' he said.

'What?'

'You're playing Janet!'

'How can I play Janet?' I said, feeling seriously worried. There were only about three weeks to go until filming started. The other actors had been going over their scripts for some time. How could he expect me to catch up?

'Do it for me, Maureen,' Gary said, his eyes shining.

Oh God, I thought. I can't! But I said yes, anyway.

That night, I couldn't sleep. I was in a waking nightmare. The same thoughts kept running through my head. What have I done? I should never have said yes. How can I do it? I was in a right two and eight.

The next day at rehearsals, my name was up on the board. It took my breath away to see it. But I'd landed myself in this. I'd said yes to Gary. I couldn't let him down. I couldn't let my nerves get in the way.

'Don't treat me no different than anybody else,' I told him, and he didn't. If he didn't like the way I did something, he said so.

Nevertheless, I was incredibly nervous. What have I got myself into? I kept thinking. I can't act! I was way out of my depth.

It was a bit of a shock to go from working in a betting shop in Catford to trying to act alongside a cast of top actors in a major film. Working with people like Ray Winstone, Kathy Burke, Edna Doré and Jamie Foreman was intimidating. I was in awe of them. These were people I watched on the telly and admired. I didn't feel I belonged among them. I don't think they knew the film had parallels to my life when we started out, but they must have realised later on, when we got to know each other and talked about our lives – although we never directly discussed it.

Luckily, I got on with everyone in the cast. We really bonded during the rehearsals and filming; it was like we were one big family. Ray's a diamond, anyway, and so is Kathy. They're all fantastic people and we totally gelled. Whenever Charlie Creed-Miles was about, I'd say, 'Here's Billy, my boy.' It made a difference that everybody was so nice.

Knowing how difficult I was finding it, they all helped and supported me. We'd do a read through and if I wasn't getting it, they'd make suggestions as to how it could work. 'Try it this way,' they'd say. I was really grateful.

It also helped that I was playing a role that was so close to who I am. Even though everything I said was scripted, the dialogue was true to me. It was still hard to speak it, though. Once I knew my lines, I had to work on the tone of each scene: 'Can you make it darker?' Gary would say. That sort of thing. It was a crash course in acting.

We filmed over three months, in November, December and January, 1995–6. The first scene I did was the one where my son Billy turns up at the factory where I work. There were so many lines to learn. I was petrified.

'What you doing here?'

'Have you got any money?'

'Don't be silly! I gave you money this morning. What you done with it?'

'Well, something come up. You know what I mean? I had to fucking weigh off a mate of mine.'

'What mate?'

'A mate, Mum. I owed him a bit of dough.'

'Well, I ain't got any money!'

'Oh, Mum, don't fuck about!'

'Don't raise your voice at me and show me up at fucking work. How much do you want?'

'A score.'

'I haven't got a score! I don't go to fucking work so that you can spend it on your fucking mates! What have you done with the money I gave ya?'

'I've done that, ain't I?'

'What, on fucking gear?'

'Don't fuck me about.'

'Do you know how much money you've had out of me over the last fucking year? It adds up to fucking thousands.'

'Don't be stupid, thousands. How do you work that out?'

'Because you've got a sixty pound a day fucking habit and I've been supporting it, like some cunt!'

'Just lend me a tenner, then.'

'I haven't got any fucking money!'

And so on. It was a really long scene and the thought of trying to get it right overwhelmed me. How would I remember my lines as well as knowing where to walk and what to do while I was saying them?

The night before we filmed the scene, I tossed and turned in bed, dreading what awaited me the next day. When I got up in the morning, my heart was pounding. My stomach was turning over. I had diarrhoea. My hands were clammy. My mouth was dry. I was sure I would be sick at any moment.

Just before we were about to start, I had a complete crisis of confidence and burst into tears. Once I'd started, I couldn't stop. I sat in the Winnebago and I cried my eyes out. This has all been a terrible mistake! I thought. What was I thinking? I can't act. I'll go out there and mess my lines up and mess the filming up. I'm going to sod everything up!

Gary came in to see how I was getting on. I took one look at him and buried my head in my hands. 'I can't do this!' I sobbed.

'Yes, you can,' he said. 'You know you can do it.'

'No, I don't think I can,' I said. 'But I've got to, ain't I? Because everything has been set up and you're waiting for me to start.'

There wasn't a choice. I had to pull myself together and get on with it. Somehow I did it, and I don't think the scene needed too many takes before it was ready to print. The funny thing is, I can still remember all the lines to this day. They're stuck in my head for good now, I reckon.

Every scene was a challenge. I ignored the cameras, but I was still completely out of my comfort zone. We did one particular scene in a working men's club, where I was drinking a vodka and tonic. There was a lot of verbal to remember, a big chunk of dialogue, and I wasn't looking forward to it. In fact, I was terrified.

'Is it all right if I have a real vodka and tonic?' I asked Gary.

'Yeah, all right.'

Well, I had about four. That did the trick.

Gary used his own tricks to get the best out of me. He'd say, 'Let's do a major rehearsal.'

Because it was just a rehearsal, I'd be relaxed and the scene would flow. When it was over, he'd say, 'Right, that's it.'

'What do you mean, that's it?'

'We took it and it was great!' he'd say, smiling.

'I thought you said it was a rehearsal!' I'd had no idea the cameras were rolling.

'Well, it's done now. Let's move on.'

I felt a lot easier after a couple of months had gone by. I really began to enjoy myself. We did a few scenes that were cut in the edit, but that didn't matter to me – it was still great to rehearse and film them. There was a particular scene I loved, when Kathy Burke, who played my daughter, was doing my hair.

'I wish I could help all them poor people.'

'What do you mean, poor? We are poor!'

'Yeah, but all those people out in Africa.'

The dialogue was so well written that it felt like proper banter. After a while, it just came naturally.

The film has a lot of swearing in it, with the word 'cunt' being used more than in any other film in history, apparently. I think the swearing makes the film darker and more intriguing than it would have been without it. If there had been no swearing, it would have been a total loss, because when people get upset and angry, they tend to swear. It wouldn't have been real without it.

You can use swear words in so many different ways. You can say, 'Shut up, you silly cunt,' and it means nothing. Or you can say it in a rough, nasty way that has a far more serious meaning. It's all down to the way you say it. I don't swear as casually as my character does in the film. If a situation calls for swearing, then I'll swear, but I don't do it in my everyday conversation. I do it all the time when I'm driving, though. I eff and blind a lot when I'm on the road, because there are so many effing stupid people out there!

One of the elements that makes *Nil by Mouth* stand out is the soundtrack. The incidental music and the songs fit it perfectly. One of my favourite scenes comes near the end, when Janet's mum gets up in the club and sings 'Can't Help Lovin' Dat Man'. Gary asked our mum to record it and he dubbed her version over Edna Doré's performance.

When she starts singing, it always reminds me of the singsongs we used to have at Nan's house. It's such a sad moment in the film, because you know when you hear it that Val is thinking about Ray as she listens to it. 'Can't Help Lovin' Dat Man'... A few minutes later, the film credits roll to the sound of the Andrews Sisters singing 'Bei Mir Bist Du Schön (Means That You're Grand)', which always brings to mind Mum and Shirley and the times they got up and sang at the Five Bells pub.

A few of the tracks are co-written and performed by a singer called Frances Ashman, who also performs 'My Heart Belongs To Daddy' in the nightclub scene towards the end of the film. Me and Frances met on the film and got on really well. We're still friends today; she makes the most delicious Caribbean food in London. Seriously, her curried goat is something else.

There's an amazing coincidence at the heart of our friendship, and Frances's involvement in *Nil by Mouth*. None of us realised it at the time, but we later discovered that Dad's apprentice at the bauxite plant in Jamaica in 1956 was actually her father! What are the chances of that happening?

When we finished filming in early 1996, there was a wrap party in the West End. It was a good knees-up. We were all pleased that the film was 'in the can', as they say. I was proud of myself for rising to the challenge and it was great that Gary was pleased with my performance. I was feeling extra happy because I'd just been paid. It was fantastic to have some money, for a change. I spent it on a new car, a deposit for a flat in Bermondsey and I treated everybody to a nice holiday. Basically, I knocked it out and then went back to work in the betting shop.

Money slips through my fingers. Always has, always will. If I won the lottery, the cash wouldn't last long, however much it was. I'd buy boats and planes and helicopters, a house here, a house there and I'd treat the family. Gone!

I'm one for living in the moment. You may say, 'Let's go on

holiday next year.' But you might not live till next year. I say, 'Let's do it tomorrow, or next week!' I don't want to wait.

Due to Gary's numerous acting commitments, post-production on *Nil by Mouth* was staggered and ultimately took more than a year. During that time, I decided that my name would be listed as 'Laila Morse' in the credits. I didn't want people to know that Gary was my brother, and assume that I'd only got the part because of him. I wanted people to judge my acting on its own merits, not because I was his sister. A lot of people didn't know about our relationship at the time – and even now they express surprise when I tell them.

It was Isabella Rossellini who came up with the idea for my stage name – using an anagram of *'mia sorella'*, which means 'my sister' in Italian. Gary did the anagram part and suggested 'Laila Morse'. Job done.

Along with the rest of the cast of *Nil by Mouth*, I went to a screening of the film when it was finished. I was proud of the part I played in it, but I found it really sad to watch. I couldn't help crying, especially when I saw that Gary had dedicated it to Dad: 'To My Father'. I cried because it was a really moving film, but also because I was seeing a version of my life on screen. It was a film but it felt so real, and brought back so many hard memories. Sitting beside me during the screening was my sister Jackie, tears streaming down her face.

'What a powerful film,' I said to Gary afterwards. 'I think it's absolutely wonderful.'

The strength of the writing, acting and directing stunned everyone. But did I think it would be popular and win awards? No. I could never have predicted that, perhaps because I was so close to it. I started to get an idea of how successful it would be after it was screened at the 1997 Cannes Film Festival. I didn't go to Cannes, but it soon became obvious that *Nil by Mouth* had caused a stir. The reviews were absolutely outstanding and the next thing we knew, Kathy Burke had won the Best Actress award. The film was a sensation.

The critics loved it. 'Shot and scripted in a deceptively casual, bleakly "realist" style, it's the closest Britain has produced to a Cassavetes film, and as such, profoundly humane,' *Time Out* said. Other British reviews were equally positive.

Even the American critics responded to it, after the film had opened in the States. 'Rough, tough but with an underlying generosity toward its characters, Gary Oldman's *Nil by Mouth* is an impressive writing–helming debut cloaked in a torrent of profanity and loutish, abusive behaviour,' said *Variety*. Janet Maslin in the *New York Times* actually singled out my performance: 'An episode in which Janet drives Billy to make a drug buy and watches her son shoot up, helpless to make his life any better, presents the film's pathos at its most searing.'

The critic at *Variety* also had a lot of praise for the cast. 'Winstone, a former boxer, dominates the film with an intensely focused performance that perpetually carries the threat of physical violence ... Both Burke, as his punching-bag wife, and Morse, as his tough mother-in-law, inhabit their characters' skins, with Doré contributing a sparky cameo as the fearless grandma. Of the other men, Foreman is very good as Raymond's raconteur pal, and Creed-Miles fine as the withdrawn Billy.'

'You'll be in demand after this!' people started saying. 'You can act professionally.'

'Leave off, I only done it for Gary,' I said. 'I've no intention of doing anything else. That's it for my acting career.'

Life went on as normal. Then I had a phone call from Ray's agent, Michael Wiggs, the managing director of Creative Artists Management. He said he wanted to see me. I went to meet him at his office in Shoreditch.

'You're good,' he said. 'You were fantastic in the film.'

'But I'm not an actress,' I said.

'You are if you want to be,' he replied, smiling. He said he wanted to sign me up. I was gobsmacked.

He put me up for a job on *The Bill*. I went along to the audition and read out a section from the script. 'Can you cry on demand?' the director asked me.

'I can, but I'm not going to now,' I said.

'Why not?'

'I've got my make-up on,' I replied. 'I don't want to smudge it.'

To my amazement, I got the part of Janice Ryan, a confidence trickster. She only featured in a couple of episodes, but I liked playing her. I still didn't give much thought to whether I wanted to become a full-time actor, though. I'm that sort of person: I can take it or leave it.

Luckily, my boss at the betting shop was good about letting me have a few days here and there to do some acting, so I did a few bits and pieces after that, including a bizarre pilot for a really strange sitcom called *Honky Sausages* for the UK Play channel. The show follows the adventures of an extremely weird, often obscene family. I play the mum. The father is a black man who sits in front of the telly and eats boiled eggs and honky sausages. The daughter has twelve kids, all by different blokes. There are three sons: a white son who is a pimp and two black sons, one a gangster and the other a womaniser. Like I said, bizarre!

In one of the scenes, the womaniser son is about to shag an old biddy of ninety. 'Would you like a honky sausage sandwich?' I ask her.

'Not now, dear, I'm going to be too busy.' When I give her a puzzled look, she goes on to say, 'Yeah, I've got some Viagra and I'm going to fuck like a tiger!'

In another scene, my youngest son is sawing off his warts and yelping with pain. 'What's the matter, honky son one?' I ask him.

'I've got all these warts...' he says.

'Yeah, from too much wanking!' I tell him.

It was a very strange script, but I enjoyed making it, especially as we were allowed to ad lib quite a lot. The cast and crew were a nice bunch of people, so it was a good experience for me. The writer wanted to take it to America, but it didn't happen in the end. It's a shame, as I would have liked to make more episodes.

In October 1997, *Nil by Mouth* had its premiere in London. It was really exciting. Thanks to Gary, I'd walked down a red carpet before, but this was different, because I was actually in the film. I felt proud as I walked into the cinema in Leicester Square, with Gary, Ray, Kathy and the rest of the cast. Jackie and Gerry were by my side. We were all looking forward to the after-party, which was being held in a private club.

I found it hard to sit through the film again, partly because I get fidgety if I have to stay still for too long. I think it got too much for Gerry, because he got up halfway through, went out to the bar and got talking to Eric Clapton, who composed the film score. They struck up quite a good rapport. Eric is a recovering addict. 'Any time you want to speak, give me a ring,' he said to Gerry.

Tracy didn't come. When she tried to leave Brooke with her bloke for the night, Brooke screamed so much that Tracy felt she couldn't leave her. It was a pity, but her mothering instinct was stronger than her desire to go to a film premiere. She's seen it since, of course. She thinks it's brilliant.

It was around this time, to my relief, that she took her chance when her partner went away for a few weeks and finally left him, once and for all. She never went back, although they made friends again later on down the line. She doesn't hate him – and, to be honest, neither do I, even after all that's happened. She feels sorry for him, because he's not very well now. It's a sad ending to a sad story, but at least he has a good relationship with the kids.

Tracy struggled to set herself up alone, but she made it work this time. She went on to meet someone else: Jason, the son of an old school friend of mine. She first met him when he did some painting at a friend's house. Afterwards, she had him at hers to do some tiling. Then he went to a neighbour, then to me. He's very good at what he does.

Tracy liked him, but when one of her friends said that she thought he fancied her, she didn't know what to do. She'd only ever had one boyfriend until then. Nothing occurred for a long time, because Jason wasn't prepared to step in until he knew for sure that her relationship had definitely finished. Finally, he came back to do some work on the house for her and one thing led to another. They started going out together.

I was so happy for her. I approved of Jason. He was really nice and gentle and I knew he would look after my girl. 'What's your intentions, then?' I asked him jokingly, one day. 'Are you moving in with her, or what?'

'She ain't asked me,' he said, hesitantly. That was that. He moved in.

Everyone was pleased that Tracy had made a fresh start with someone new. Meanwhile, my relationship was going from bad to worse. Jim was boozing more than ever and we constantly argued about his drinking. He got on my nerves when he drank too much. He'd say the same stupid thing over and over again.

We still had fun sometimes, but I couldn't stand the lies he told about not being drunk. He became crafty about hiding bottles. He was always trying to conceal his drinking.

'I've only had one,' he'd say, when I came in from work.

'Don't tell lies! You've had six!'

If someone is truthful with you, then you're far more likely to accept their behaviour than if they blatantly lie to you. His deceitfulness wound me up so much. It drove me mad! I don't like liars.

Things came to a head on the night of the BAFTAs in April 1998, almost three years after I'd married him. *Nil by Mouth* had been nominated for several awards and everyone was excited at the prospect of the evening ahead. Me and Jackie were set to be on Gary's table. Jim was going to join us for the knees-up afterwards.

I must have had an inkling that things would go wrong, because I was worried about Jim coming even before I left the house. 'Don't you dare turn up until the awards are over!' I warned him. 'Come at around eleven.'

It was a triumphant evening for Gary. *Nil by Mouth* won the Alexander Korda Award for the Best British Film and a BAFTA for the Best Original Screenplay. We were over the moon as the ceremony unfolded. Everyone was celebrating. There were disposable cameras on the table and we snapped away delightedly. At one point, Jackie took a picture of me and Gary with Michael Caine in the middle of us.

Me and Jackie made sure we didn't have more than two glasses of wine. We drank water for most of the ceremony, because we didn't want to be on the boozy side when we went upstairs for the after-party. All these big stars were up there, including Michael Caine, Helen Mirren and Judi Dench. To my dismay, so was Jim, my drunkard husband. Ignoring my warning, he had turned up early and started knocking the drinks back. By the time I went up there, he was as drunk as a sack. It was disgraceful.

'I told you not to get here till about eleven!' I said, unable to hide my frustration.

He went around making a right nuisance of himself, as he often did when he was drunk. Eventually, I lost my temper and fisted him in the face.

Gary was in a side room being interviewed. Suddenly, Jim burst through the door, shouting, 'Your sister's just clumped me!' It was so embarrassing.

We weren't there fifteen minutes before we all walked out: Gary, my mum, Jackie and me. Me and Gary didn't speak for a long time over it. Jim ruined everybody's night, but particularly Gary's, and it was his big BAFTA night! To make matters worse, Jim lost the camera with all my photos of the evening.

Just a Mo

I really hated him after that. That's it now, I thought. I don't want to be with you any more. I stopped sleeping with him; I didn't want anything to do with him.

The rest of the year was really up and down for me. Things were generally good, but the state of my marriage constantly brought me down. In October, me and Jackie and Mum went on holiday to LA. It was a relief to get away from Jim. I was seriously thinking about leaving him by then.

The three of us had a lot of fun in America. One afternoon, the phone rang. Mum picked it up. It was Gary, ringing from London. 'What's he doing phoning at this time?' Jackie said. 'It must be past midnight in England.'

'It's those awards tonight, isn't it?' I said casually. My heart started thumping.

'What awards?' Jackie asked.

'The British Independent Film Awards.'

I heard Mum say, 'Wait, I'll put you on the loudspeaker.'

Suddenly, we could all hear Gary's voice. 'Tell Mogsy that she's won the Best Newcomer award in all categories!' he yelled. 'I've just picked it up on her behalf.'

'Blimey, who'd have thought it!' I said, bursting into happy tears.

'Isn't that wonderful!' Mum cried, giving me a hug.

'Yeah!' I said, sobbing. 'Yeah, it's bleeding wonderful!'

chapter eleven

Mo Meets Mo

I WAS AT Mum's house when my agent rang me. When I put the phone down, I swear I was several shades paler. 'What is it, Mum?' Gerry asked me.

'They want to audition me for *EastEnders*,' I said, feeling completely stunned. I felt like a rabbit in headlights. 'But I don't want to!'

'Mum, it's an opportunity. Go for it,' he said.

'It's all very well for you to say, but you're not the one who has to do it!' I yelled at him. The phone call had put me in a right state.

EastEnders? Was it a joke? I was a big fan of the show. I've always loved the soaps, from *Coronation Street* and *Emmerdale* to *Holby City*, which isn't strictly a soap, but is absolutely brilliant nevertheless. I had watched *EastEnders* from the very beginning, so I was really involved with all the characters and plot lines. But I was involved as a viewer, not an actor. How could I, an amateur, be expected to hold my own alongside all those seasoned professionals?

I was a novice. I hadn't been to acting school, like they had. I was totally naïve about what was expected of an actor on the set of a major soap. I wouldn't have a clue what to do! The sum of my experience was *Nil by Mouth*, *Honky Sausages* and a bit part in *The Bill*. I had also played Molly, the woman who Pip saves from the gallows, in Channel 4's *Great Expectations*, and a bit part in the crime comedy,

Love, Honour and Obey, which starred Sadie Frost, Jude Law, Jonny Lee Miller, Ray Winstone, Kathy Burke and Rhys Ifans. It had all been good fun, but I was only playing minor parts.

Now I was up for *EastEnders*? It was madness. There was no way I'd be good enough.

'It's only an audition,' Gerry said. 'You might not get the part.'

Strangely, that calmed me down.

The audition took the form of an acting workshop in which we played out different scenarios and began to develop our characters. 'Maureen "Big Mo" Harris is the head of the family and she does a bit of wheeling and dealing,' the director told me.

I know people like that! I thought. I have friends who wheel and deal a bit. So it was easy to identify with the character sketch they gave me and I began to create the role of Mo in my mind. It just came instinctively; I had hardly any guidance as I brought out how I thought she would be. I must have got something right, because the director liked the character I created. It's funny to think that Mo is still doing her bits and bobs to this day, trading with Fat Elvis and people like him, getting a load of knocked-off gear and selling it.

'How would you feel if you were in *EastEnders*?' I was asked at the workshop.

'I don't know,' I said dismissively. 'Take it or leave it, I suppose.'

I'm not the type of person to say, 'Ooh, I'd really love to do it!' What you see is what you get with me. I suppose that helped me to get the part in the end.

When I did get it, I rang up and said I didn't want to do it. 'Nah, it's not my cup of tea,' I said.

I couldn't admit that I was feeling overwhelmed by fear and insecurity. The truth was that I still didn't think I was good enough to do it. I kept thinking about all the people who had been in *EastEnders* for years. How on earth could I match up to them? I didn't want to be in the show for a couple of weeks and then get booted out. So I told myself, and the producers, that I didn't want the part. But I got it anyway – and I've been there ever since!

The one thing I asked was that the name be changed, because I'm known as Mo by some people. 'I'm afraid it's already been decided,' they said.

'Can't you change it to Maud, or Pearl, or some old-fashioned name?' I said. But, no, they kept it as Mo.

Mo's return to Walford, after nearly forty years away, had an immediate impact on the local community. Entering the fray with her son-in-law Charlie and four granddaughters, her first big storyline featured Pat Butcher. Mo and Pat had once been the best of friends, but they fell out after Mo married Pat's older brother Jimmy and had two children with him. Later, Jimmy died of cancer, but not before handing Mo a note to give to Pat, saying he'd forgiven her for the past. Pat never knew what was in that letter, to the day she died, because Mo never gave it to her. She still has it in her drawer somewhere.

So my first big scene was with Pam St Clement, a.k.a. Pat Butcher. Pam is a lovely, talented woman and we got on really well, but I was petrified at the thought of acting opposite her. Working with people I'd watched on the TV every week was very strange and intimidating. Making the transition from viewer to cast member was every bit as hard as I'd thought it would be.

The scene was set in the square and was full of recriminations, which meant that my debut in the show definitely wouldn't go unnoticed. I would be coming in with a bang, appearing in an explosive scene opposite one of the show's big stars, and a great actress into the bargain. Mo and Pat hadn't seen each other for years; suddenly, here they were, practically neighbours. I can't remember the lines now, because it was so long ago, but one of them said, *'I'd like to bury the hatchet.'*

'What, in my back?' the other shot back.

I was shaking with nerves before I went on. I had all the same symptoms that I'd experienced on *Nil by Mouth*: the sweaty hands, the feeling of nausea and that awful sense of terror. My stomach was flipping over like a live kipper. 'I don't think I can do this,' I told Pam.

She gave me a big, confident smile. "Course you can. You know your words, don't you?'

'Yes, but...'

'That's all you need. You'll be fine!'

I can't remember doing the scene. It went by in a haze. I was so relieved when they said, 'Right, check that!' and gave me a thumbs-up.

I thought I was a bit stiff when I watched myself back, though. A couple of weeks later, a TV critic said I acted like a lump of cardboard, and I dare say he was right. I was new at the game and I was bloody petrified. It's not surprising that I was as stiff as a board! It was a good two or three years before I started to feel comfortable on the set. Until then, I couldn't do a scene without my stomach turning over and my hands getting sweaty. Even though I knew my lines off by heart, my mind would often go blank when I got in there and did it.

It happened once with Steve McFadden, who plays Phil Mitchell, in a scene where he came to sell me some knocked-off fish. I couldn't get it right, because I was so intimidated by the thought of working with him. I got myself in a right two and eight.

When they said, 'You're next,' I'd stand there shaking as I waited for my scene. I was petrified. A lot of people say it makes your performance better, but I don't know about that. Either way, I prefer not to feel sick.

For years I couldn't sleep the night before a scene. I'd lie in bed, going over and over the lines in my head. Some people find it easy to learn lines, but I didn't. It can be even harder to deliver them. I really admire actors who make long speeches without sodding up. I've sat through many a scene on the telly or in a film, wondering how on earth they did it. Did Kevin Costner, in *JFK*, manage to do his famous speech about Kennedy in one take? I can't believe he did. Twenty-five minutes talking without making a blunder? Surely it can't be done. I don't care how bleeding clever you are.

I got over my nerves in the end. It's like everything. Take driving, for instance. When you first go behind a wheel, you're terrified. After a while, your main worry is whether you're going to pass your test. Once you pass, you find you're scared to go on the motorway. Eventually, driving comes automatically and you think you can drive with your eyes shut!

It was like that with acting on *EastEnders*. I slowly built up my confidence. Now I just do it and if I sod up a line, I do it again. I've realised that everyone makes mistakes. If they say they don't, they're lying, because I've seen them. I've watched all of the other *EastEnders* actors mess up at one time or another. Big movie stars are the same, I'm sure. They don't get it right every time. That's why films take so long to make.

One day I realised, Blimey, I don't feel nervous any more! The nausea wasn't there. My heart wasn't pounding. I felt relaxed. It was a massive relief. I still have a bit of a problem in that I like to work in silence, though. I can't focus when people are sodding around, laughing and giggling. It puts me right off my stroke. I'm one of those people who has to concentrate; I suppose it's my age. Apart from that, I can act with my eyes shut, just like I can drive! I know my character inside out now. I can switch her on and off. As long as the director is clear about how to play a scene, it's not hard to get it right.

You record the show seven or eight weeks before it transmits, so although I was working and going in and out of the studio, no one knew who I was until the first episodes were aired. The first time I appeared in the show was on 18 September 2000 and not long afterwards I was named 'Arrival of the Year' by the *Sunday Mirror* TV critic Ian Hyland. I was really surprised and thrilled.

After a while, people in the street started shouting out, 'Look, it's that Mo out of *EastEnders*! Mo! Mo!'

It made me feel weird. 'You're going to have this for the rest of your bloody life,' said one of my friends, after I was recognised in the car.

'Give over,' I said. 'I wouldn't like that.'

I thought back to the fortune-teller predicting I'd be

famous one day. Was this what he had foreseen as he inspected the lines on my palm? I remembered how people had laughed at the very thought of me becoming well known. How strange life is.

Fame didn't go to my head. Instead, it went to my husband's head, unfortunately. Ginger Jim lived off my name and went around telling anyone who would listen who I was. He worked all over the country and sometimes when he was away, he'd ring me up at three in the morning to get me to say hello to a barmaid.

'You know who I'm married to?' I'd hear him say. 'Big Mo in *EastEnders*! Don't believe me? Here, you can talk to her.'

'Say hello, Mo,' he'd say, passing the phone over.

'Fuck off!' I'd shout. 'Go and sleep with him, or something!' It did my head in, especially when I had to get up at dawn to go to work the next morning.

Jim was getting worse and worse, boozing and behaving like an idiot. He never hit me, but I gave him a few digs, especially when he said he hadn't been drinking and it was obvious that he had. It was all so silly. But after a while the situation deteriorated to the point where it became clear that there was nothing more I could do.

He often embarrassed me when we went out. He'd get drunk and show me up, just like he had on the night of the BAFTAs. I was fed up with him anyway, but I was especially sick of having to make excuses for him. I can't be having you in my life now I've got a different lifestyle, I thought. How can you take a boozer like that along to a smart do?

The writing had been on the wall for a while, but then something happened that made my mind up to leave him, once and for all. We were walking along the street in

Bermondsey, on our way to a pub, when all of a sudden I caught sight of Jimmy on the other side of the road. My heart went over, just like it had the very first time I saw him.

Twenty years on from our fantastic holiday in Ibiza, Jimmy looked as handsome as ever. Mesmerised, I watched him as he stopped to speak to someone he knew, his face breaking into the beautiful smile that I remembered so well. In that moment, I realised that my feelings for him hadn't changed. The magic was still there.

'Come on, Mo, stop dawdling. Let's get the drinks in,' my husband whined.

I turned to look at him. Not once, I thought, has my heart turned over at the sight of you. You don't make me feel like he makes me feel and you never have. That was the last nail in the coffin of my marriage. I made Jim sleep in another bedroom from that day on.

A couple of months later, I rented a flat in Bermondsey and applied for divorce papers. I filled all the forms out, describing Jim's behaviour and why I couldn't stay with him. His mum got on the phone and created something terrible. 'Why are you saying this about him?' she asked.

'Because it's true!' I said.

I took the papers up to him and got him to sign them. He didn't argue. I think he must have seen it coming. That was that. No money passed hands. I dare say I broke his heart, but there was nothing I could do about it. Sometimes these things happen in life. Anyway, it was his own fault. It was a relief to be shot of him and I swore never to get married again.

I don't know why I made such bad choices when it came to my relationships. I don't analyse why I do things, I just do them. So I find it hard to find a reply when people ask, 'Why did you stay with him?'

It was a sad end to an unhappy episode in my life, but I needed to put the past behind me and start afresh, especially when I heard that Jimmy, my Ibiza love, had got married. My heart sank when I was told that particular piece of news. I suppose I'd always had a secret fantasy that one day we would get together again. Now, it wasn't a possibility. He was married. I'd lost him for good.

Fortunately, I was almost too busy to dwell on Jim or Jimmy. My time was filled with my work and my mates and I wasn't interested in meeting men or dating. That was all over for me, as far as I was concerned, especially as the one man I had feelings for was unavailable. I threw myself into my friendships instead, and my mates filled up my spare time.

I was still seeing a lot of my old pals Jan and Karate Sue; I'd also become close friends with Tracy Norman, who lived in the flat below us at Deptford Wharf. We'd bonded over our dogs: my dachshund Sundee and her two little westies. We'd got talking one day as we were both coming down the communal stairs, and often chit-chatted after that. Then I asked her up for a drink in my flat and she asked me back down to dinner at hers, and soon we became good friends. Tracy Norman used to work in a bank, but she now works for one of the top London auctioneers. She's the same age as my Tracy and we call her Tracy Norman to differentiate them. Even when I took her to America and we went to see Gary, he said, 'Hello, Tracy Norman!' using her name in full. She doesn't mind. She's got used to it now.

My gay friend Russell is another important mate. I became friends with him when I rented the flat next door to his in Bermondsey, after I'd moved out of Jim's place. It all started one boiling hot summer's day, when Russell and his partner had a huge load of old railway sleepers delivered. I happened to look out of my window and saw them lugging these great big things into their flat and out into the garden, where they were planning to lay them. Poor sods! I thought, so I took them out two cold glasses of wine. We got chatting and became good friends after that. In the years that followed, Russell often came with me to awards ceremonies and events when I was invited with a friend. A retired social worker, he is really and truly funny. He gets on with everyone and makes us all laugh so much. We've had some brilliant times together, out at parties, on holiday – and just sitting at home with a cup of tea.

My other close friends are Martin and Stella. I've known Martin since we were kids, when he was a saucy little thing living at the end of Hatcham Park Road, back in the late 1950s. Our families were good friends then and kept in touch over the years. Martin was younger than me, but you level out as you grow up, don't you? When he and Stella got married twenty-two years ago, they lived around the corner from Mum in New Cross. His brothers and sisters all moved away, but he stayed in the area and so we remained good mates. There's nothing like friends who have known you all your life.

Naturally, I also made a load of new friends at *EastEnders*. We were all introduced when the Slater family first went on set and it wasn't long before I palled up with people. I became very friendly with Wendy Richard (Pauline Fowler), Derek Martin (Charlie Slater), Gillian Wright (Jean Slater), Laurie Brett (Jane Beale), Shane Richie (Alfie Moon) and Jessie Wallace (Kat Slater). Shane and Jessie cracked me up all the time. Jessie is constantly laughing and when she laughs so does everyone else. Shane is really funny. There's never a dull moment when he's around and if anybody's down in the dumps, he'll always make them laugh. He's got a great sense of humour and he's a very clever actor.

June Brown (Dot Cotton) was another big character behind the scenes. June's a really lovely lady with a great sense of humour and she's constantly making people chuckle. You can never get a word in, because she's so full of stories about all the things she's got up to and all the different acting jobs she's done. She chats like there's no tomorrow – but she's such a good storyteller that you could listen to her all night. We were both guests of John Bardon, who plays Jim Branning, at his wedding in 2002, and as soon as I saw I was sat next to her for the wedding breakfast, I knew I was in for a treat. Oh, we had a right laugh. I was in stitches for most of the evening.

About a year after I started on *EastEnders*, the Queen and Prince Philip visited the set and came down to meet everyone at the Queen Vic. We were all told what to do and how to address the Queen. I shook her hand, curtsied and said, 'How do you do, Ma'am?' It was a real honour to meet her and everyone was chuffed. Not a lot of people meet the Queen! I was struck by how beautiful she is; she's got a face like porcelain, a really lovely complexion. I'm not a royalist, but I like the royal family. Not many countries have kings and queens, so I suppose we're lucky.

There was a real sense of fun and camaraderie behind the scenes at *EastEnders*. When you got in, you'd plonk your stuff down and go straight to the green room, the area where you could sit and relax before going on set. Wendy Richard would often get in early and when I arrived she'd be sitting there with her cigarette holder between her fingers. We'd smoke our cigarettes and chat, have a coffee and a bit of breakfast. Even people who didn't smoke would come and join us. There was a smoke-free green room, but everyone congregated in ours.

There was so much laughter back then. We all gelled, because we were there every day. When it was time to start filming, a runner would come and look for you. 'Mo, you're on now!'

At lunchtime, someone would go on a fish and chip run and we'd all sit in the green room with our fish and chips, salt and vinegar. We'd have a laugh and take the piss out of the things that had happened that day.

There was always so much going on. In 2003, a dozen or so of us were asked to do a spoof of the Michael Jackson *Thriller* video for Children in Need. We learned the dance routine in a couple of hours and performed it out on the Square. Shaun Williamson (Barry Evans) played Jacko and Lucy Speed (Natalie Evans) was his date. I was a zombie – and quite a convincing one at that, according to my family!

I enjoyed the times when we just got on with our normal routine, too. Hanging out in the green room, talking about this and that, was always good fun, and us actors sometimes went through our lines together as well – which often turned out to be really helpful. Once, I was going through my script when I came to a word that I couldn't make out. 'What's a kwish?' I asked Wendy. 'Or is it kwyshe?'

She laughed. 'It's a quiche!' she said. 'As in quiche Lorraine.'

What an idiot I am! I thought. But she found it funny.

I loved Wendy. We first bonded over her little dog called Shirley. We used to call her Shirley-whirly and other silly names. Once, when Shirley had a grass seed in her foot that was really troubling her, I said to Wendy, 'I've got some time off. I'll take her to the vet for you.' Wendy thought that was kind and we became good friends after that.

Wendy was very dry, very comical, and constantly making me laugh. She was also very kind-hearted. She did a lot for charity and one day she told me she was planning to do a charity run. 'Do you want to do it with me?' she asked. 'We'll get halfway round and have a drop of medicine!'

Medicine? I thought. It turned out that she only drank Moët champagne – and she called it her medicine. 'Fancy a drop of medicine?' she'd say, towards the end of a long day on set.

'Yeah, all right,' I'd say. She always had some Moët in the fridge in her dressing room. Everybody knew it was all she drank, unless it wasn't available, in which case she would make do with very good wine. At the *EastEnders* dos, there would always be Moët on ice for Wendy.

We became very close. She came to stay at my mum's one Christmas and a few times I went with her and her husband John to Malta, where she had a place. Like me, she loved a bag and shoes. Wherever we went, she'd say, 'Ooh, look at that! Nine hundred pounds? I like that. I'll have that!' She liked her jewellery as well.

We went to lots of dos together, and on outings. I became a Lady Taverner for the Heritage Foundation through Wendy; she recruited me. The Heritage Foundation runs a charity called The Arts and Entertainment Charitable Trust, which raises money for good causes, including children with disabilities. Wendy and I supported a lot of their events, going to the dinners and bidding at the auctions. I used to enjoy all that. We had a laugh. I bought all kinds of bits and pieces at the auctions, including some fantastic framed photographs of the Beatles, the Bee Gees and Norman Wisdom. Wendy also persuaded me to go to shows and the theatre, which I'm not generally all that fond of, because I get restless in my seat. One outing I did enjoy was when we went to see Leslie Grantham playing a detective in a show up in Birmingham; Wendy, Jan and me all went. It was great. Leslie is absolutely brilliant, a far cry from his character in *EastEnders*. He's funny and really talented.

I loved Wendy to pieces. She was a phenomenal woman, a really kind, loving person. I've never known anyone like her. Like many others, I was devastated when she died in 2009. Hers was the only funeral I've ever been to, apart from my dad's. I still miss her very much and think of her every day.

I was grateful to her for being such a wonderful friend, but I also had another reason to be thankful to her, because if it weren't for Wendy, I might well not be here today.

Just after Christmas in 2001, I was outside doing some gardening at home when Karate Sue called me in to see something on the television. My hands were wet and I dried them on my top, brushing the sides of my breasts as I did. 'Oh!' I said. 'I can feel a lump.' I touched the area again. The lump was wobbly; I could move it.

'You'd better go and get that checked,' Sue said.

'Nah, I expect it's only a mammary gland,' I said. 'Don't worry about it.'

When I went to work the next day, I mentioned it to Wendy. 'You need to get that checked up,' she said, frowning. She told me that she'd had breast cancer in 1996 but had been clear of the disease since then.

'I will do,' I said.

'You should make an appointment now,' she urged.

'Yeah, I will.'

'I'm going on holiday tomorrow,' she said. 'When I get back, I want to hear that you've been for a check-up.'

I took no notice. I didn't want to know. I'm not one for operations. I don't like needles or being put under, so I just wanted to ignore it.

The day Wendy got back from holiday, she rang me. 'Have you been to the doctor?' she asked.

'Yeah,' I lied.

'What happened?'

'It turned out to be nothing to worry about,' I said, evasively.

'Oh, really? That's good, then.' She didn't believe me, but she didn't say so.

If she hadn't asked me about it, I think I would have stayed in denial. But her phone call prompted me to do something. As it happened, I was going to my GP to have my blood pressure checked that week anyway. The doctor went through all the usual rigmarole and concluded, 'It's normal.'

'Thank you,' I said. I stood up to go. And then, just as I was leaving the room, I added carelessly, 'Oh, by the way, I found this lump, here.'

He called me back into the room at once and examined me. 'I'm going to write a letter of referral,' he told me firmly. 'You'll hear direct from the hospital about an appointment.'

I didn't say anything to Wendy. She didn't mention it again; she knew me well enough to leave well alone. A week later, I had a mammogram and some blood tests, and then went back for the results the following week, with my friend Jan. A professor of oncology showed me the mammogram results and talked me through them, explaining what it all meant. A lot of it went over my head, but his conclusion certainly didn't.

'You have breast cancer,' he said. No nonsense.

'Oh, really?' I replied. Strangely, I didn't feel upset by this news.

Jan, on the other hand, burst out crying. 'What are you crying for?' I asked her. 'If you've got it, you've got it. One of us was going to get it.' My approach was very accepting. I never worried. I didn't cry. I didn't tell my mum or anyone else, apart from Tracy.

The professor then said, 'We're going to take a biopsy.'

'What, now?' I said, stalling for time. I wasn't stupid; I knew it would probably involve a needle. 'I don't think I can have it done now.'

'Well, we'll have to do it at some point. Why not now?'

'It ain't gonna hurt, is it?' I asked. I'm a real coward when it comes to needles and injections. 'I'll only do it if my friend can come in with me and hold my hand.'

'All right,' he agreed.

Petrified, I lay on a bed, with bright lights shining above me, waiting for the doctor. Someone came along and numbed the skin around the lump. Then the professor arrived and produced a big needle. I squeezed Jan's hand hard. I was so scared I could hardly breathe. The needle clicked as he took the sample from the lump. Unfortunately, it didn't work the first time. 'Oh no, I'll have to do it again,' he said. Click, click. It didn't hurt, but I hated the idea of it.

'You'll hear from us,' the professor said, when he'd finished. That was that.

Funnily enough, I was less anxious about the cancer itself than about how it would affect my job. I hated the thought of it interfering with my work and I was worried that I might get the sack if I had to take time off.

Back at work, I finally said to Wendy, 'I need to speak to you.'

'What is it?' she said.

'I've got breast cancer. But I can't go and tell the people upstairs, because they'll sack me.'

'No, they won't!' With that, she marched me upstairs and made me tell them, there and then.

I blurted out my news to the producer. 'Does that mean I've got the sack now?' I asked, not really wanting to hear the answer.

'Don't be silly,' said the producer. 'We'll do everything we can to work around your hospital appointments.'

And so, just ten days later, I went into hospital and had a lumpectomy. They also took away the lymph nodes from under the arms. I can't remember much about that time because I've blocked it all out. As I've said, I can't stand anything to do with hospitals. I just wanted to get it over with and carry on with my life.

I had a week in hospital, a week at home and then I went back to work, still padded up under my clothes. After that, I had to go to the hospital twice a week to have the fluid drained off, but I felt fine. I had radiotherapy and that was it. Done.

'You're lucky,' the doctor said. 'It's hormonal.'

'It's more than likely down to those tablets I've been on,' I said to him. As he knew, I'd been taking HRT for three years to top up my oestrogen levels after the menopause.

He wouldn't comment. I took that as a yes, especially when he suggested I stop taking HRT.

I started taking the breast-cancer drug Tamoxifen and then, once I had healed, I went for six-monthly and then annual check-ups. Ten years down the line, I don't have to go any more. It's done and dusted. I'm thankful for that, of course I am. But I can honestly say that I never, ever worried about the cancer or what the consequences of it might be, because I'm a great believer in fate. I didn't think I was going to die, but if I did … well, there was nothing I could do about it, was there? I think your life is mapped out from the day you are born, whether you last a day, a week, a few months, five years or die as a teenager. Your number is printed and you go when your time is up, whether it's in a car crash or under a bus, whether you get cancer or die in your sleep aged ninety-nine. When your time is up, it's up.

I'm good at blanking things out. It was only when I'd got the all-clear that I even told my mum I'd had cancer. And after that, I put it out of my mind. I don't even think about it now – although I can't deny that I'm glad I'm here to tell the tale. It really makes me sad that other people haven't been so lucky, especially my lovely friend Wendy, who I still miss so very much.

chapter twelve

Fame and Fortune?

AFTER YEARS OF having to penny-pinch, borrowing here and there to make ends meet, buying things on the never-never and often going without, suddenly I had money coming in. It was fantastic. I had a lot more money than I'd ever had in my life. It felt great and it still does, even though it just slips through my fingers.

You'd think I'd have loads of money stashed away after twelve years of being in a programme like *EastEnders*, but it hasn't worked out that way. I should be saving it for a rainy day, but as I've earned it, I've spent it, always putting enough aside for my taxes first. I like to spend money. My priority is helping out my kids and grandchildren with cash when they need it. I also enjoy treating people and buying presents.

You never know when you're going to die. Why risk leaving your money to the government? I don't like what the government stands for or the way they treat old people, so I begrudge giving them a penny. I've never voted in my life. I don't vote and I won't vote. I don't care about politics. None of the politicians stick to their promises. They're just wooing you over; it's like a romance, when someone promises you the world and ends up giving you nothing. Our only great prime ministers were Margaret Thatcher and Lloyd George. They looked after the people. I wouldn't give you two bob for anyone else.

Having money is great, but it hasn't been trouble-free. In the first place, it lost me a couple of friends who went on the turn when I started in *EastEnders*. Instead of being pleased for me, they were jealous. 'A new settee?' they'd say pointedly. 'New blinds, *again*?' That was that. You can't be friends with someone who turns green every time you see them.

Another problem with having money is that people try to wheedle it out of you, usually by selling you something. There are some dodgy dealers out there. So when I started thinking about buying an apartment in Spain, I was careful to go with someone I trusted.

My sister Jackie had some friends who were planning to move to Spain to manage rented apartments for tourists and sell real estate. When they moved out there in 2004, I told them I was looking for somewhere to buy. They said they could help me in my search. Since I'd met them a few times with my sister and they seemed like good people, I was grateful for the offer.

They had a fabulous apartment along the coast from Benidorm and I was keen to explore the area, so when they asked me to stay I went out to see them quite a few times over the next eighteen months. They always made me welcome and we got on well. I felt I could trust them or, at least, that there was no reason not to trust them.

Unfortunately for me, they must have seen me coming, because they ended up asking for a loan, then borrowing more than they asked for and never paying me back, which left me more than 10,000 euros out of pocket. I felt so betrayed. I had trusted these people and they had repaid that trust by taking me for a ride. I look back and wonder if they thought that I had money coming out of my ears because I was on TV, but I doubt it. They knew me better than that. No, I think they simply took advantage of my trusting nature, and I found the whole thing very hurtful.

I've become a lot more wary of people's motives since that particular episode, which is a bit of a shame, I think. Still, it was partly due to them that I eventually found a lovely apartment to rent in Spain, because our falling-out led to me exploring a different area altogether and I fell in love with an apartment on that resort instead. As it happens, my friends Martin and Stella visit there often, as Stella's sister has a place on the same resort, so it all turned out for the best. Every cloud has a silver lining, as they say.

Losing ten grand to so-called friends was a blow, but I was able to absorb the loss, because I was still earning. At least I had a good accountant, who was keeping my finances in order. A friend of mine in the business had recommended someone; let's call him Tony. Tony did the accounts of a lot of actors, so he knew the industry inside out.

Whenever I was paid at work, I put a percentage away to pay my tax at the end of the year. Tony would calculate how much I owed and I made a point of sending a cheque to the Inland Revenue the very next day.

So I was surprised when I received a tax demand for £1,000, a few months after I'd paid what Tony had told me was due. I rang him up to ask what it meant. 'Don't worry, you don't owe anything!' he assured me. 'It's a mistake.'

'How do you know it's a mistake?'

'Don't fret. This sort of thing happens all the time.'

A month later, another demand came, for £2,000. I rang Tony again. 'Disregard it!' he said. 'Trust me, I've got it all under control.'

More demands came. I couldn't get hold of Tony to ask him about them, but I wasn't too bothered. I had total faith in him and he had told me not to worry. A few weeks later, there was a knock at the door. I opened up, expecting the postman. It was the bailiffs. They said I owed money to the taxman. I slammed the door. 'I've paid my tax!' I called out to them from inside the house. They knocked again. I ran to the phone to ring Tony. He didn't answer.

The bailiffs came again. I couldn't understand it. I had regularly sent cheques off to the Inland Revenue. Why were they saying I owed them money? Then I had a letter saying that, if I didn't reply by a certain date, I'd be taken to Holloway Prison and kept there until such a time as the judge wished to see me.

'You need a solicitor,' Jackie said. 'And fast.'

I hired a solicitor, who did some research into Tony. It turned out he was only a bookkeeper, not a qualified accountant, which meant he wasn't up to the job. My solicitor also found out that he was living abroad. His UK office, where he supposedly worked, could only be contacted through mobile phone numbers.

Tony didn't answer any of my solicitor's letters. He wouldn't give up any of the paperwork that I'd sent him for all those years. Meanwhile, the bailiffs kept coming round. I was in Shit Street.

My solicitor found out that Tony's daughter had died, which maybe explained why he never got back to us. I felt sorry for him on a personal level. Of course I did. But your work goes on. If you can't do it, you get someone else to do it. You don't just leave people high and dry. He got me into terrible trouble with the tax man. My outstanding bill was forty grand. With interest and penalties for non-payment, it shot up to sixty-six grand. As a result, instead of being all right for money, I was thousands and thousands of pounds in debt, all because Tony didn't do his job properly. Why did he keep saying I didn't owe money, when I obviously did? As a result, I'm going to have to pay hundreds of pounds in back tax every month for the next ten or fifteen years! My solicitor says I could nick him, but no one can find him. Someone will tell me where he is before long, though. I just need to find out where he lives.

So here I am in debt, and yet a lot of people assume that I've got bundles of money because I'm on the telly. It doesn't half piss me off sometimes.

I'll be buying something in Boots and someone will come up and say, 'What are you doing shopping in here?'

It's such a ridiculous question. 'Where do you think I'm going to shop, bleedin' Harrods?' I snap.

'Yeah, with your money!'

It winds me right up. 'Hold on a minute,' I'll say, 'the tax man and the VAT man take my money. I ain't rich, not by a long chalk.'

Most of the time, I don't mind being approached by people when I'm out and about. I can't help smiling when I'm walking along and a busload of schoolkids passes by, banging on the window like mad, screaming, 'Mo! Mo!' It makes me feel like a pop star! I always wave back and say hello.

Unless I've got the hump, I say yes to people when they ask for autographs and pictures. Mostly, I'm happy to sign a book or pose for a photo and I'm never rude if I can't do it. 'Not at the moment, I'm sorry,' I'll say. 'I'm a little bit upset,' or 'I've had bad news.'

It can be annoying when you're out to dinner and people don't wait until you've finished eating before they come up and talk to you. I don't want to be interrupted in the middle of my dinner by someone asking for an autograph. It's tempting to say, 'No, you can't! Piss off!'

Since I don't want to be put in that position, I tend to go to local restaurants, where no one bothers me and I know I will be left alone. I'll talk to people and have a picture done, all well and good. But let me eat my food!

Being approached does become a bind; it can get on your nerves. So I always go to the same Sainsbury's up the road, where I know people are not going to bother me. Someone or other might say, 'Hello, Mo!' or wave, but they don't stop me now, because they know I'm local.

When people say, 'I love being recognised,' I wonder if they really do, because most of the time I don't. It can be especially difficult when you have people asking silly questions like, 'Where's Kat?'

'How would I know?' I say, with a forced smile.

Some people really think that you are a bloody family! 'Are you out shopping with the Beales today?' they ask. It's really hard to know what to say to that.

It's nice when people come up and compliment your work, though. I see the actor Owen Teale at Sainsbury's quite a lot. He's done a lot of different television work, in anything from *Robin Hood* and *Ballykissangel* to the more recent *Stella* and *Kidnap and Ransom*. One day, we were both at the checkout and he said hello. 'I love your work!' I told him. 'Yeah, and I like yours, too,' he said. That was that. We both went home feeling good.

Most of the time, people approach me and say nice things, but I had a nasty episode with a so-called autograph hunter back in 2008. Karate Sue was staying with me at the time.

She'd eventually got away from the demanding partner she'd had when we lived next door to each other, thank God. He later died of a tumour on the brain, which might explain why he was a bit odd. Sue moved out to near where her mum lived in Broadstairs and that's where she's been ever since. We stayed in touch, though, and she used to come up to see me almost every weekend.

This particular night in June 2008, she was sleeping in the back bedroom of the house. It was a hot summer evening and the window was open, although she didn't realise quite how wide open because it was hidden by a fully drawn blind and curtains. At around 4 a.m., she was woken by a noise outside. Normally she would have just assumed it was my cat Drexel trying to get in, because he used to sleep on her bed sometimes. But, this time, something pulled her out of bed and drew her to the window to investigate.

As she got closer, she heard a thump. She thought that Drexel might have fallen off the glass roof of my lean-to, which was just below the window. Poor old cat, she thought. Since she was stark naked, she wrapped herself in one of the curtains and pulled up the blind so that she could see outside.

But instead of my cat, there was a big bloke at the window, about to clamber through it. In another second or two, he would have been inside the room. As soon as he saw her, he crouched down. He had a knife between his teeth.

'What the fuck are you doing? What do you want?' she yelled at him.

'I want Mo's signature,' he said.

'There's no Mo lives here!' she said, furiously banging on the window. 'Now, piss off, before I call the police!'

At that, the bloke fell backwards onto the roof of my lean-to and then rolled onto the ground. He was hobbling when he stood up. 'I'll be back for you,' he shouted, shaking the knife at her. 'You've broken my ankle!'

Gerry was asleep in the room next to Sue's. He woke up to the sight of her running through the door with no clothes on, shouting, 'Someone's just tried to get in the window!' I was sleeping in the front room and didn't hear a thing. My little dog Eric was asleep on my bed and he didn't hear anything, either. It was strange, because he's usually very sensitive to noise.

Sue woke me up and told me what had happened. We called the police at about 4.30 a.m., but they didn't send someone over until lunchtime the next day. 'You took your time,' I said, when they finally arrived.

They apologised. The local station was stretched to the limit by a horrific double murder that had taken place a couple of streets away in the early hours of the morning.

Sue told them what had happened the night before. 'Can you describe this man?' one of the constables asked.

She started telling him what she could remember about him. The constable frowned. 'You say he was hobbling when he left the premises?' he asked. 'Excuse me a moment, I need to contact the station.'

Sue's description of the intruder matched that of one of the men who had been involved in the double murder a couple of streets away. It turned out that he'd gone directly from my house to a bedsit nearby where two French biochemistry students lived. He stabbed them 244 times, in what was later described as 'an orgy of bloodletting', and afterwards he tried to set fire to them.

Sue had to give a witness statement to the police. They went down to Broadstairs to interview her and the whole episode was brought up in court during the murder trial, a year later.

I had slept through the entire incident, oblivious to the danger, and unless something has happened to me, I don't worry about it. 'Right, we can't have the window open any more,' I said to Sue.

Still, I appreciate that we probably had a very lucky escape. 'He definitely wasn't coming in to have a cup of tea,' Sue said grimly. 'If he'd got in, he would have deaded us, good and proper.'

'But he didn't, because you woke up and gave him what for,' I said. 'You deserve a medal for that. 'Course, if he'd come any further, you would have floored him with a karate chop!'

I was joking, but I was well aware that if Sue hadn't woken up thinking she could hear Drexel at the window, neither of us might be here today. It's a terrible thought. I also realised that if I wasn't well known, he probably wouldn't have bothered us. But there's nothing I can do about that now. Even if I was sacked tomorrow and I couldn't get another job in the industry, people would still know me. 'Weren't you in *EastEnders* once?' they'd say. My card is already marked!

I love my job and I feel very lucky to be doing it, but I don't care about being famous. For a short while after I joined *EastEnders*, I went to all the dos and awards ceremonies. I don't bother with them any more. I can't stand that red carpet stuff. Some people love it and glory in it, but I haven't been to an awards ceremony for eight or nine years. If I could go in the back way and leave the back way, then I might think about it again. I much prefer to do stuff behind the scenes, and I'm lucky to have had some great opportunities come my way over the years. I've never lost my fascination with film sets, and so when Tim Monarch, Gary's dialect coach, invited me onto the set of *The Good Shepherd* in 2006, I jumped at the chance. Tim has worked with Gary on a few of his films and I've known him for fifteen years or so, so it was good to see him again and catch up. I had lunch with Tim, met Matt Damon and a few of the other actors from the film, and went home. It was a nice day out, and so much more interesting than an awards ceremony.

What I don't like is getting out of the car at a fancy event and being greeted by photographers saying, 'Hello, Laila! Can you turn to the left? Turn to the right?' You hang around while they take picture after picture and then the only photos they print are of the youngsters! It's such a waste of time. I can't be dealing with stuff like that.

I'm not a big-headed person. If it all ended tomorrow, I'd simply go out and get another job. I'd miss the money, but I'm someone who accepts the cards life deals me. When something happens, it happens. I wouldn't be one of these people who says, 'I have to do something in the business.' If need be, I'd go back to the betting shop or get a job in a pub. Just as long as I could entertain people and make them laugh, I'd be happy with whatever I did.

chapter thirteen

Daughter, Sister, Mother, Nan

I SOMETIMES THINK it would be good if Gary did a follow-up to *Nil by Mouth*, showing what happens to people like us as time goes on. It's funny to think how we've all turned out, now the years have passed. Take our mum, who is now ninety-three! Mum's amazing. She still knits, does crosswords, plays Scrabble, cooks and makes pies. And she is still based here with me and my sister Jackie, in the family home where we've all come and gone for the last forty-five years.

The house is full of memories. At times, me and my kids, Jackie and her kids and Gary and our mum all lived here together. Gary was surrounded by women as he grew up, which perhaps explains why he gets on so well with them.

Mum goes out to see Gary in America every now and again. I miss Mum when she's away, but it's good to know that she's having a great time in Los Angeles. She's met loads of nice people there and belongs to a club of mums whose sons and daughters are actors. Tom Selleck's mother is the chief of the group. They hold parties and dances, which is fun for Mum. She goes out to the cinema and theatre quite a lot and has become very good friends with Millicent Martin, the English singer and comedienne from Romford, who now lives permanently in the States. Mum even goes once a week to feed the homeless when she's out there. She's on teas and cakes.

Me and Gary live our separate lives and do our separate things, partly because he lives on the other side of the world.

We don't ring each other and we just meet up when we meet up. But he's still my brother. People ask me what it's like having a film star in the family, but I don't think of him how I think of Matt Damon or Robert De Niro, because he's my Gary. I'm used to his world now. When I see how he lives, I don't feel gobsmacked in the way that I used to. I suppose that's partly because I'm in the industry as well these days.

Gary married Donya Fiorentino fifteen years ago and they had two gorgeous boys, Gulliver and Charlie. They didn't stay together, though, and three years ago he got married to Alex Edenborough in Santa Barbara. He and Alex restated their vows a year later in Somerset and all the family were there. It rained and rained until an hour before they went to the church, when it brightened up and stayed gorgeous. We had a good time. It was a nice crowd of people. The drink flowed and the food was delicious. Gary has been married four times now, but I think he's got it right this time and I'm really happy for him.

I've been out to America to visit Gary several times in the last fifteen years. Me and Jackie went for Mum's eightieth birthday. Gary planned it; he threw a party for her on the *Queen Mary* ship in Long Beach and flew us out. Mum knew nothing about it until she saw us at the party. We surprised her by coming out from behind a curtain, singing, 'Sisters, sisters, there were never such devoted sisters,' by the Beverley Sisters. We stayed out there for a fortnight. It was fantastic.

I took my granddaughter Brooke to LA eleven years ago, when she was ten. Tracy Norman came with me another time, as has Russell. I also went with Wendy Richard, before she died, and I went with Frances, the singer in *Nil by*

Mouth, for Mum's eighty-ninth birthday. I didn't go for Mum's ninetieth, because Gary took her to Las Vegas, where they stayed in a hotel for a couple of days and went to see shows like Cirque du Soleil.

I've been to Las Vegas, but I didn't really like it. I generally don't do shows, not even over here. As I've said, I don't like the theatre. I can't sit for too long in the seats. I start fidgeting and jiggling my legs; I want to get up and walk out. I'd sooner wait for a film to come out on Blu Ray than see it at the cinema. Then I can lie on the sofa and watch it in comfort.

I made an exception when I went to the premiere of *The Sweeney*, starring Ray Winstone, in September 2012, breaking my rule about avoiding red-carpet events into the bargain. I could hardly sit out the film, though. Even though it was very entertaining, I wanted to get up and go because my legs were so restless. Still, I went because I wanted to say hello to Ray. I hadn't seen him in ages.

'Hello, Mo!' he boomed, in his warm, friendly way. He was there with his family and it was really nice to see them all. His girls were only little the last time I saw them; they're all grown up now and they looked lovely. Charlie Creed-Miles was also there. He was wearing very dark glasses and seemed a bit reticent, but I gave him a big hug.

It was nice to go out and we had fun at the after-party, but I tend to stay at home much more these days. Perhaps it's something to do with getting older. Mind you, there's never a dull moment in our house, what with the kids and grandkids coming and going, and my lively little dog, Eric, constantly getting over-excited. Eric is seven now. He's gorgeous and I love him to bits. He's the best dog I've ever had. He behaves himself and happily walks beside me when he's off the lead. And he's so clever that he understands what we're saying – so sometimes we have to spell things out to fool him. For instance, I'll say to Jackie, 'Do you want to go for a W?' so that he doesn't go mad at the thought of leaving the house. The problem is, he's even worked out what that means!

My sister Jackie is really easy to hang out with. We get on well, even though we're as different as we ever were. She was always the quiet one. Unlike me, who left school and did about a hundred jobs in two years, fifteen-year-old Jackie got a Saturday job at a hairdresser's and later trained as a milliner over the West End, a job she stayed in for some time. She didn't flit around like I did.

We both went down the same road by getting pregnant young and having to get married, though. After Jackie divorced, she brought her girls up herself. There was no one like George in her life. My nieces, Lesley and Sally Ann, are nice kids. I call them kids; they're married with their own children now. Jackie didn't meet anyone for years and years. But now she's with Sean, who she's been seeing for twenty-two years. He's a great guy and they have a good relationship. They shared a home for a while and, although they live separately now, they're still friends and go out from time to time.

Her life hasn't always gone smoothly, but Jackie is more stable than I am – and when she puts her mind to something, she does it. We call her Jack-A-Fix-It, because she can fix anything. I can't work a computer or a laptop. I have an iPhone, but all I can do is ring and text people, whereas Jackie can fix plugs, plumb in the washing machine, set up the TV and DVD. She's just one of those people.

I say, 'Jack, get on Amazon for me, please, and order so-and-so.'

'Why can't you do it?' she complains.

'You know I can't do it! You can, so you do it.'

That's how it's always been. It's not because I'm lazy; I just think that if someone can do something for me, they may as well do it. You don't have a dog and bark yourself, do you? These days, I pay people to do my windows, or paint the front room. I could do it myself but I don't, because I'm in a position now to employ people to do the bits and bobs. I suppose if I wasn't in this job, I'd be doing it myself, because I'd have to.

I'm constantly changing things around in the house. Every two or three weeks, I'll move the furniture around in the front room, or swap a bedroom over so that I'm sleeping in the front instead of the back of the house, or vice versa. I've painted my kitchen walls an array of colours over the years; sometimes I have them redone after only two months. I like change. I don't know why it is, I just do. It's the gypsy blood in me, I'm sure. I'm restless. I've lived here, there and everywhere. I couldn't tell you half the places I lived. If I had enough money to travel wherever I wanted to whenever I wanted to, I'd be in a different place every week.

I think my Gerry probably takes after me. He's a bit of a restless character, too. He's had periods when he's settled down, but then he's up and off and into trouble again. He was in prison again recently. It was a pity, because after decades of being in and out of the nick, he'd vowed never to go in again. I did my best to help him stay out, because I knew how much he hated it. It cost me an arm and a leg, sometimes £1,000 a month, because it meant giving him money to stop him nicking stuff. Since I started at *EastEnders*, I've given him more money than I can count. I don't even want to think about how much it adds up to. That's what I mean about money slipping through my fingers.

It couldn't go on forever; it wasn't doing either of us any good. Everything came to a head one night in 2011, when Gerry crept into the house, took my car keys, nicked my car and trashed it, all while I was asleep. The insurance company refused to cover me for the damage, because they don't pay up if the car is written off by anybody you know, anyone who works with you or lives at your house. So, even though the crash had nothing to do with me, it cost me ten grand out of my own pocket to sort it all out.

I decided enough was enough. I reported Gerry to the police. He was sent away for four months. He was lucky, as he could have been given three years. No one went to see him, because he was right up in Norfolk. I've been in so many prisons and borstals it's unbelievable, but I don't do that any more. Apart from the fact that they are horribly depressing places and I hate seeing my boy locked up, I couldn't go to see Gerry now because people would clock me and, before I looked round, it would be in the papers. He understands. He knows I'd be there like a shot if he really needed me. Anyway, with any luck he won't be going away again.

Gerry cleaned up in prison and seemed all right when he came out. He's such a different person when he's not on that stuff. He's loving and clean and tidy. If he cooks himself something, it will all be washed up and wiped down after-wards, with everything put away. I had him to stay here when he came out, but it's no good living with your mum when you're forty-three.

I don't suppose it will be long before he goes back to his old ways, but you never know. I live in hope, but it's day to day with him. What can I do? I feel as helpless as I ever did. I can't change him. He does his own thing. It's what he does. It's all he knows. You can't tell him anything. He's all right, though. He's a survivor. I suppose we all are. You've just got to keep going.

As for my daughter, everybody thought Tracy would get pregnant after Jason moved in, so it was a surprise when she didn't. A friend of hers had just gone through the change in her late twenties, so Tracy wondered if she was menopausal at the age of thirty-five. 'Go and get checked out,' I told her. I knew she wanted another baby, even though she was saying she didn't mind either way.

She had some tests and was diagnosed with polycystic ovaries, which explained why she'd never had regular periods. She took a fertility tablet that helped her ovulate and three months later, she became pregnant with Jess, her third child, who was born ten years ago. Jess was a very lively baby and I think Tracy found her quite hard work. When she and Jason spoke about having another one, she told him she felt too old to go through it for a fourth time.

But five years later, while we were on holiday in Spain, I started wondering if she could be pregnant again. We were eating chorizo sausages in our villa and she was tucking in like nobody's business, going on and on about how delicious they were and how much she loved chorizo. In the end, she ate so many that she was sick! 'I think I might be pregnant,' she told Jason, when we came back from holiday.

'Don't be silly!' he said. 'It's not possible without those fertility tablets.'

Jack was born seven months later, a clever, naughty child. He was Tracy's third Caesarean and I think the birth and its aftermath affected her health quite badly. She already had health problems after suffering whiplash years ago, when someone drove into her while she was out in her car. Since Jack was born she's developed terrible problems with the discs in her back, among a host of other complaints. She's got so much wrong with her now. She's in constant pain and takes morphine tablets; she's put on weight and has days when she has to stay in bed. As a result, she's not really the person she used to be – and I miss the slim, fun-loving Tracy she once was. It worries me.

Still, she stays positive. Like Gerry, she's a survivor. She's a great mum and she and Jason have a very nice relationship. He's her soulmate. They do everything together and he never goes out without her. He can see what a great person she is and he respects her in every way. I couldn't be happier that she's with him. I'm very close to Tracy and I always have been. I feel really lucky to have a daughter who is also my best mate.

I'm lucky too, in that I'm close to all my grandchildren; I love them to bits. If I can help them in any way, I will. If they want anything, I'll get it. I'm always treating them, every single one.

Happily, I still have a special relationship with Brooke. We have a lot in common. She reminds me of me when I was younger, which is more than likely why we have a bond. We like the same things, especially handbags and shoes, and we've both got big bums!

I often had Brooke with me when she was young. As I've said, I took her to restaurants from the age of one and she would always be prepared to try something new. Even today, she'll eat all the hottest dishes, full of garlic, spices and chilli. When she was about five, I taught her how to use chopsticks. I also used to doll her up like Madonna and teach her Madonna songs. She'd sing, 'Like An Urging' instead of 'Like A Virgin' and make everyone laugh. She was always a good little kid, whereas her younger sister Jessie is as good as gold when she stays with me, but as soon as she's with her mum, she's a nightmare, continuously naughty.

While we were on holiday together in Spain last year, Brooke decided to get a tattoo done on her leg. She got back home on the Monday, had it done on the Tuesday and texted a photo of it to Tracy on the Wednesday. It was a beautiful design of Japanese lilies curling up her thigh. I loved it the moment I saw it. I'm a big fan of tattoos, anyway; I've got about five now.

'I want one of them!' I said, as soon as I saw it.

'Nan,' Brooke said. 'Do you have to get the same as me?'

'Why not? You're my granddaughter!'

'Yeah, but *exactly* the same one?' she asked.

'I won't have dots on mine, then,' I conceded. I went and had it done on the following Thursday.

Brooke softened when she saw it. 'It means something special, because we've both got it,' she decided.

'It looks far better on me, though!' I joked, and we both fell about laughing.

chapter fourteen

Never Too Late

'HELLO, HOW ARE you?' I said to Jimmy. I hadn't clapped eyes on him in five years. Now here we both were in Tesco in Bermondsey.

He smiled one of his big smiles. My heart turned over. I had to remind myself that he was married. 'I'm all right,' he said. 'How are you?'

'All right, just come back off holiday,' I said, as casually as I could. I'd been out in Spain for three weeks with Tracy, Brooke, Danny, Jessie and Jack. We'd had a lovely time and I was feeling healthy and tanned.

'Yeah, you look well,' Jimmy said, still smiling warmly. That was that. We said goodbye and went our separate ways.

A few months later, I'd just finished having my nails done in a shop in Bermondsey when I saw him outside on the street. I paid my bill quickly and went out to say hello. 'All right! How are you?' I said, trying not to show my excitement.

He frowned. 'Actually, I'm not well,' he said.

I inspected him more closely. He looked tired. 'What do you mean, you're not well?'

He shrugged. 'I don't know what it is, but my legs have been hurting me.'

'Oh dear,' I said. 'Give us a ring if you need any help, will you?' I gave him my telephone number. 'I mean it,' I added.

'All right,' he said.

That November, while I was away on holiday, my phone rang. It was Jimmy. We had a chat about this and that. My heart thumped through the whole conversation. 'Are you better?' I asked. 'Did you find out what was wrong?'

'I've been diagnosed with thrombosis,' he said. He didn't go into it, but I gathered that it was quite serious.

'I'll be coming home in a few days,' I said. 'I'll come round and see if you need any help.'

When I got back, I went to see him. He wasn't well at all and couldn't get around because of the pain in his legs. To make matters worse, he was allergic to the medicine that people usually take for thrombosis and the only alternative was to have injections in his stomach, every day, for six months. It was a miserable time for him.

Although he was still married, he wasn't living with his wife. I don't think they'd ever lived together. It suited them better to keep separate homes. I felt sorry that there was no one to look after him, so I started doing a bit of shopping for him and ran him here and there in the car when he needed it. We became very close friends. But that's all we were, friends. We didn't take it any further, although I would have liked to. I still felt the same way about him and was hoping something more would happen, but we both knew it wasn't possible while he was married.

Eventually, several months down the line, one thing led to another – of course! The first night we spent together was just like our first time in Ibiza. We were reliving what we had then, but it was better, because we're older. Afterwards, I was walking on air. My stomach turned over every time the phone went. It was brilliant. I felt like an infatuated teenager.

'I've always loved you, deep down, for all these years,' Jimmy told me.

I was so thrilled. 'Me, too,' I said shyly.

It was something that had been inside me all that time, but I didn't talk about it and sometimes I didn't even think about it. Life went on and then I'd hear a song or see a film that reminded me of the ten days we were together. Little did he know that seeing him on the street in Bermondsey had effectively ended my marriage. He knows about it now, but I didn't give everything away at once!

'I often thought of you after the holiday,' I said. 'I wanted to leave George...'

'You should have come over and knocked on my door,' he said.

'But I didn't know where you lived.'

'I was only opposite the pub. You could have found me.'

'Yeah, but things was different in them days.' Meaning, I hadn't had the confidence to try and find him. I was too scared of rejection.

'What happened to George?' he asked.

'I don't know,' I said. I've heard since that George has been really unwell.

Jimmy told his wife we were seeing each other. She caused murders and uproars. She accused us of having an affair for a long time, but it was a load of cobblers. I hadn't seen him since before they were married.

She divorced him and we're now together. He loves me to bits and I love him to bits. He calls me 'my one and only, my true love' and he is my beloved in every way. I couldn't be happier. Sometimes I feel like he is the only person I've ever loved, although I know I once loved George too, to begin with, anyway.

Me and Jimmy are good together. We get on really well. We don't live together: he stays with me quite a bit; he stays at his own house in Bermondsey quite a bit; and we go on holiday quite a bit. Getting married is not on the agenda. I like it as we are. When you're married, it all goes pear-shaped.

Our life together is happy and uncomplicated. We go for walks – or 'W's! – with my little dog Eric. We like to go to galleries to look at art. Jimmy likes churches and watches historical programmes. He won't miss *Homes Under the Hammer* for anything. We enjoy going on holiday and sunbathing; we often go out to eat. We stay in a lot, too. I like cooking; he likes cooking; we enjoy good food. I still love my roast dinners. I do a roast about three times a week: roast pork, beef or chicken with roast potatoes and three or four different veg. Other days, I'll do sausage, mash and onions, spaghetti bolognese, stuffed hearts, stuffed marrow, liver and bacon, ham, egg and chips, bubble and squeak, cold meat and pickles, all that type of stuff.

Everyone in the family likes Jimmy, especially the grand-kids. They call him 'Jimmy Two Shoes'. Little Jessie came up with the nickname. I haven't a clue why, but it fits.

Spain is one of our favourite places to spend time. I rent an apartment overlooking a golf course in Murcia, Alicante, on the same resort that my mate Stella's sister has a place, which makes for a really social holiday. The flat has two bedrooms, two balconies and a nice big kitchen and front room. I love it there. Me and Jimmy have made some really good mates out there called Jack and John; they look after us like a mum and dad, even though they're only our age. They come and pick us up at the airport and take us shopping to the supermarkets and the Sunday markets. We go and eat with them. They'd do anything for us and we're very fond of them. We often arrange our trips to coordinate with Martin and Stella, when they go and stay at Stella's sister's place. Oh, the four of us have had some great times together in Spain.

I feel very lucky to be with Jimmy. Who'd have thought it? It's a proper turn-up for the books! I could never have predicted it, not in a million years, although now we're together it seems obvious that we were always meant for each other. I wonder if my nan could have seen it in my tea leaves, or if Jas's cousin could have found it in the lines of my palm? I believe in fate, as I've said. I think your life is mapped out for you. So I wonder if I always knew on some level that we would be together one day. Maybe that's what made my heart turn over so violently the first time I saw him. Who knows? I just thank my lucky stars that we bumped into each other again and that, this time, the stars aligned and brought us together at last.

It shows that it's never too late to find love and fulfilment. After years of frustration and disappointment in relationships, I thought it was all over for me and romance. I didn't have a clue that the best was yet to come! So you should never give up on love, because you don't know what's around the corner. It can happen when you're least expecting it and in the unlikeliest places. Tesco in Bermondsey? It's not Venice, is it?

Who'd have thought I'd be madly in love at my age, and who'd have thought I'd still be in *EastEnders* now, twelve years after my first appearance with Pam St Clement? Did I hear someone say that life begins at fifty?

Pat and Mo had some funny times together before Pam left the show. There were lots of scenes where they had a laugh. But when Pat was dying, I found it really hard not to cry. There were some really tear-jerking scenes, although the comic side of Mo refused to lie down. One of my favourite scenes was where Mo visited Pat in hospital, when she was close to death. I loved doing it, although I had to hold back the tears. I willed myself to keep it together.

'You're a tough old bird, Pat,' Mo says worriedly, after Pat has a terrible coughing fit. *'Whatever it is, you can beat it, can't you?'*

''Course I can,' Pat replies gruffly.

'I'd best be going,' Mo says. As she reaches the door, she turns and says, *'You keep that chin up.'* She pauses. *'All three of them!'*

I really enjoy acting when I'm given a good storyline, but a big one hasn't come my way for a long time. When the Slater family first arrived, we had quite a lot to say. I also had a nice bit of a storyline to work with when Mo had a boyfriend called Bert. Then there was the time Mo delivered Sonia's baby in the front room, as well as all the drama around the various Slater weddings. But I've not had anything that I can get my teeth into for a while now and sometimes it feels like my character is drifting through the show. Still, Mo has two brothers, and a son and a daughter who haven't been introduced yet, although perhaps it's too late for all that now.

Mo's a big character and I really enjoy playing her. She will never stop wheeling and dealing. I'd like to see her get her house back and reunite with her two brothers. I'd also like one of her kids to knock on the door, and for the script to introduce more grandchildren. It would be great for Mo's family to cause chaos again. They would turn the Square upside down.

Either way, it's good working at *EastEnders*. I love being in the show. I keep myself to myself much more than I used to, though. Over the years, I've seen a lot of people come and go and there aren't so many people who have been there a long time now. A lot of us don't know each other. I preferred it when I was first there.

The biggest change has come about because of the smoking ban. Frankly, it's not like it used to be when you could smoke in the green room. We were all friends and gelled back then, but no one goes into the green rooms any more. Most of the time, we're in our individual rooms, which are like pigeonholes. When it's time to go on set, instead of runners coming to find you, you just get a phone call to your room. Often, we only come out when we're going on set or want something to eat or drink. I might have a quick chat with someone if I go up to reception to get a cup of tea. Then I'll go straight back to the pigeonhole.

'Hey, I haven't seen you for ages!' someone will yell, and then I won't see them again for weeks.

If you want to see people, you have to hang around in reception, where everyone goes before they head off to Stage 1. Loads of people seem to stand down there and chit-chat or go outside and have a cigarette. I don't do that. I stay in my room, read, watch my telly and learn my lines. Before, you'd say to someone in the green room, 'Run through those lines with me, will you?' Now, you don't see anybody to go through your lines with, or not until you get on set.

Over the years I've been a guest on a few chat shows, like *Paul O'Grady*, *Alan Titchmarsh*, *Graham Norton* and *Loose Women*. I like doing them, even though I'm naturally shy. People don't believe that I'm shy, but I am. I suppose the way

I speak covers the shyness. It's a front I put on. It means that no one can tell when my insides are churning over. What am I going to do? I think. What am I going to say?

Funnily enough, I don't get nervous before I do interviews. They don't bother me one bit. I never prepare what I'm going to say. I just come out with things on the spur of the moment; I'm quick with my answers and if they're funny, they're funny. The main thing is not to um and ah, so I'm a bit fiery with my comebacks.

I couldn't help laughing the first time I went on *Loose Women*. I had said as a kid that I'd like to be 'a loose woman in Piccadilly'. Instead, all these years later, I was on *Loose Women* not far from Piccadilly! I wonder what my eight-year-old self would have thought about that.

And I wonder what my twelve-year-old self would have thought of me appearing in *Dancing On Ice* in early 2012? I think she would have laughed herself silly at the whole idea, because although I skated in Streatham when I was around that age, you couldn't actually call it skating. It was more a question of standing up in a pair of skates and shuffling around the rink holding on to the sides!

I was approached to do the show in the autumn of 2011 and I thought, Why not? It'll be a challenge and it's good to challenge yourself. How wrong I was. I wish I'd never even considered it.

First, I had to meet Jane Torvill and Chris Dean, to answer a few questions and show them what I could do on the ice. I've never been so frightened in all my life. I couldn't really stand up on the skates. Never mind, I thought. I can improve with practice.

After getting through the first round, I started training

with a very nice coach called Wendy, who taught me how to move on skates and master some basic steps. A few weeks down the line, I decided to do some extra practice, because I was getting on quite well and was keen to improve.

That Sunday, I happened to mention to one of the producers that I was going off to the rink to practise.

'You can't go alone!' she said. 'Wendy is busy coaching, so I'll arrange for someone else to meet you there.'

Why do I need someone with me if it's on my time? I thought. But I didn't argue.

The coach they sent to meet me was a bit on the enthusiastic side. 'Can you do this? Can you do that?' she kept asking. I couldn't do any of it.

'Can you do the crossovers?' she added.

'No, I haven't got to the crossovers yet,' I said.

'Let's give it a go,' she suggested. She showed me what to do. 'Now do it on your own.'

I tried, but my toe pick got caught as I slid along the ice and my arm jerked back, ripping the rotator cuff muscles and tendons in my left shoulder. It was agonising, just agonising. I was on the floor, crying with pain. 'I've broken my arm!' I told the coach when she came over. But then I realised that I couldn't have broken my arm, because I hadn't fallen on it.

I got up, still in pain. 'Come on, let's get going again,' she said.

After ten more minutes, I said, 'Listen, I'm going. I can't be doing this. My arm is absolutely killing me.'

Back at home, I phoned the show's physiotherapist. A car came to pick me up and took me to see her. 'You've got quite an injury there,' she said, feeling my shoulder.

She sent me for an MRI scan at St John's Hospital. The results showed a big hole in the rotator cuff. All the muscles were torn. 'You need an operation on this,' the doctor said.

There was nothing that could be done until I'd been on the show, but I had to rest for four weeks, which meant I couldn't train. So I was way behind everybody else. I went to the hospital a couple of times for injections to stop the pain, but nothing really helped. I was in pain for months. It often woke me up in the night. I couldn't sleep properly. Luckily, *EastEnders* had given me three months off.

After that, I was terrified of the ice, just petrified. The next time I skated was at Christmas, when all the contestants met up and we were told who our partners were. Everyone was nice and my skating partner Lukasz Rozycki was lovely, but I couldn't do a thing, no lifts, nothing. I couldn't even lean to either side and I was in agony all over again if anything jerked my shoulder. It was worse than labour pains! I wouldn't let go of Lukasz's hand because I was petrified of falling over.

I couldn't pull out of the show, because I was contracted to appear. I'm a trouper, so I tried to smile through the pain and not show how much it was affecting my performance. But I was no good. I was voted off the first week. I was a blink of an eye in *Dancing On Ice 2012*! Still, I was glad I was voted out, because I couldn't have done anything without Lukasz. I couldn't have jumped in the air or done any backward moves.

Besides that, the other contestants were all slim and young, even Rosemary Conley. All right, she was only a bit younger than me, but she was slim! I'm quite a stocky person, so the others had an advantage from the start. I was up against dancers and ballerinas and athletes. I'm best out of it,

I thought. It was a nightmare, although I couldn't have wished for a nicer team of people to look after us.

Maybe it would have been more fun if I hadn't hurt my shoulder. Maybe I would have done all right. Who knows? I signed up to it because I thought I would enjoy it and it would be a good challenge. But after the injury, I just hated it. The thought of going on the ice was just too terrifying. A week after I left the show, I had the operation on my shoulder. I had four plastic gromits put in and they cleaned out all the debris and sewed the hole up. It was a lot better after that.

It was a relief to go back to *EastEnders*, all in all. But then in June 2012, I was called up to see the executive producer, who told me that my contract was ending in July 2012 and they weren't going to renew it.

Goodnight, Vienna, I thought.

I launched into my leaving speech, 'I've had twelve years here. I've met lovely people and I've enjoyed myself…'

'Hang on a minute!' the executive producer interrupted. 'It doesn't mean to say we're getting rid of you. We still want you in for different storylines!'

So I'm still there, but I'm not contracted, which means that if I'm busy when they want me, I'm not obliged to put *EastEnders* first. When I was under contract, I was much more limited in what I could do. Now, I can do exactly what I want. I thought it would mean I wouldn't be in the show much, but I'm glad to say that I've done quite a lot since my contract ended.

Now it was down to my agent to find me work, and he did. First, I was offered the chance to write an autobiography. I thought, Why not? I've got a bit of a story to tell.

I've done other bits and bobs. I saw Kathy Burke a little while ago when we did a voiceover for an animation about street cats called *The Feral Cats*. My cat was a bit of a dodgy, grass-smoking character. Alan Ford was another cat. I've known Alan for a long time. He played Brick Top in *Lock, Stock and Two Smoking Barrels*. Kathy played the third cat. She looked well and it was nice to see her. She hasn't altered: she still smokes and has that striking deep voice! I'd love to act with her again, but I think she likes to direct more than act now.

In the late summer of 2012, my agent rang and asked if I'd be interested in doing a pantomime. It would be a four-week run with two weeks of rehearsals; I'd be playing the fairy godmother in *Jack and the Beanstalk* at the Croydon Theatre. 'But I've never done a pantomime before!' I said. But then I thought about it. 'Well, except when I was a kid. So, all right, then!'

I didn't audition. They said they wanted me to do it and they were over the moon when I said I would. They came round my house with all the costumes and we did a photo shoot, just like that. The director seemed like a lovely guy. The whole team was very pleasant and I felt comfortable with all of them.

'How do you want me to play it?' I asked the director.

'As cockney as anything!' he said.

Well, that shouldn't be a problem, I thought. I'll just be myself, with a bit of Mo thrown in for good measure. The main thing is that I like making people laugh. If I can do that, I'm happy.

So, at the time of writing, here I am in pantomime again, more than half a century since my last pantomime appearance. The show is a sell-out and I'm looking forward to it, but I've still got a lot of anxiety, especially as my lines are all rhyming couplets. I can't get these blooming couplets into my head. I'm just not used to learning poetry. When the time comes, I'll more than likely have to have my lines written on my wand! That'll make them laugh, at least. I'll say, 'Hang on a minute, I've forgotten the words!' and make it look like it's part of the show.

I don't know whether I have to sing and dance yet, but I've said I'm not singing a song on my own. I'll probably have to sing along with other people, but I'm quite happy to do that. It's just a singsong then – like in the old days down the Five Bells, or round my nan's piano. There'll be some rousing, crowd-pleasing number to do at the end, no doubt, to send everyone on their way with a smile on their face and a kick in their heels.

I'm excited about going on stage and at the same time I'm terrified. Every time I think of it, my heart goes over. It's a big responsibility when you're top of the bill. God knows what it will be like. I haven't been on stage once for more than fifty years and I keep thinking, will I pull it off?

Well, I have to pull it off! I've signed the contract and I can't sodding back out now. That's what keeps me going. Also, I'm pleased that I've found myself another challenge, because I need to be busy and kept on my toes.

I like the idea that my life has come full circle. When I was thirteen and appeared in *Cinderella* at the Finsbury Park Empire, I was young and full of fun. I was excited about life and the future; I believed in love and family. But within a few years, everything had changed. I was trapped in an unhappy marriage, my father had left, my family was in pieces and I had lost all my confidence. The future seemed bleak, and I completely lost sight of the happy-go-lucky girl I had once been. I had to go through a lot of ups and downs ... before I finally found my way again.

Now I'm more like the cheeky kid I was all those years ago, albeit far older and a little bit wiser. I have a wonderful family. The future looks good. And I believe in love again – like never before.

Author's Acknowledgements

I'd like to thank:

Kate Moore for being a very understanding editor, as well as all the nice people at Virgin Books who have helped me to write and publish this book, including Claire Scott in publicity and Editorial Assistant Yvonne Jacob.

Rebecca Cripps for spending so much time helping me to tell my story.

Douglas Urbanski for his help regarding *Nil by Mouth*.

Gary for giving me the chance to have an acting career, and for being my lovely little brother.

Mum for always being there. You're the best mum in the world.

Jackie: we didn't always get on as kids but I couldn't do without you now, Jack-A-Fix-It!

Tracy and Gerry, my two lovely children. I'll always love you.

All my beautiful grandchildren.

And last, but not least, my lovely Jimmy.

Further Acknowledgements

Picture acknowledgements

All photographs used courtesy of Laila Morse, excepting:

Page 4 (bottom): Moviestore Collection / Rex Features

Page 5 (top): © BBC

Page 5 (bottom): Jeremy Selwyn / *Evening Standard* / Rex Features

Page 8 (main picture): Neil Genower

Text permissions

Pages 174, 176–7 and 178–9: extracts from the script of *Nil by Mouth* written by Gary Oldman © SE8 Group Ltd. Used with permission.

Page 194: extract from the 18 September 2000 episode of *EastEnders* written by Christopher Reason © BBC. Used with permission.

Page 240: extract from the 30 December 2011 episode of *EastEnders* written by Matthew Evans © BBC. Used with permission.

Index

The initials *LM* in subentries refer to Laila Morse.